KU-178-191

WINGS 4

FERRET FLIGHT

WINGS 4

FERRET FLIGHT

Charles Anthony

First published in Great Britain 1996
22 Books, Invicta House, Sir Thomas Longley Road,
Rochester, Kent

Copyright © 1996 by 22 Books

The moral right of the author has been asserted

A CIP catalogue record for this book is available
from the British Library

ISBN 1 898125 66 X

10 9 8 7 6 5 4 3 2 1

Typeset by Hewer Text Composition Services, Edinburgh
Printed in Great Britain by
Cox and Wyman Limited, Reading

1

North Korea, April 1951

Osipovsky knew he was not going to make it back to base. He was OK, but the MiG-15 was definitely not. It still flew – just – and while it continued to do so, he was getting deeper into friendly territory and away from the Sabres. Those damned Blue Fins had been everywhere.

After being fleetingly hit by the six guns of a blue-finned F-86 Sabre, he'd considered himself very lucky indeed not to have been wounded; but though it was not an immediate killing shot by the American pilot, it was still a kill as far as the MiG was concerned.

The trail of billowing smoke had grown spectacularly, and Osipovsky began to worry about getting roasted if he tried to make it back. He would have to eject. At least he was well into friendly territory now.

Osipovsky began to think of his future prospects after ejecting. He did not relish being the only survivor of the special 'Green Ringer' squadron that had been commanded by the Great Patriotic War ace Major Valentina Nerova. From the snatches of radio conversations he'd picked up, he realized to his horror that she was gone, as was Beryev, the deputy commander. The squadron had been wiped out.

He knew that the squadron had been operating under quite different orders from those of the other Soviet squadrons, all of which operated clandestinely, under 'North Korean' colours. Stalin did not want the world to know he was using the Korean War to give Soviet pilots combat experience in the jet age, and to blood the formidable MiG-15.

The Green Ringer squadron had been far more special. It had been given the best aircraft and the best pilots, whose main task was to take on the best the Americans could offer, and win. But it had not worked out that way. The best, the Blue Fins, had triumphed.

The MiG squadron's patron had been a top KGB general, who had no doubt hitched his own star to its eventual success. Given Stalin's notorious dislike for failure, Osipovsky reasoned that the general's star would soon be in serious jeopardy. That general would want a scapegoat.

'Me!' Osipovsky said aloud as the fire warning light began to blink.

He came to a decision about his own future. He would go missing in action, presumed dead. His mother originally came from one of the USSR's Asian republics and he reasoned he could just about pass himself off as a border Korean from the north-east. He was going to disappear.

Having made his decision, Osipovsky reached for the knob by his left thigh to first jettison the canopy; then he ejected.

The now-burning MiG-15 spiralled towards the ground 3000 feet below, and exploded on impact.

Osipovsky eventually landed gently, and quite unhurt.

Arizona, USA, April 1996, 10.00 hours

The two-lane blacktop undulated in a straight line across a terrain that looked more like the moon than the earth. There was a single car cruising along it, but in the far distance behind, currently in a dip in the road, was another vehicle, travelling fast to catch up.

The cruiser was a Ford Mustang. It was not new, but a '69 fast-back model. Despite its vintage, there was something purposeful about the way it powered along on its fat new wheels. This was in no small measure due to the spanking, newly rebuilt Shelby Cobra engine lurking beneath its scooped bonnet, the large tailpipes at the rear betraying the existence of the non-standard motor.

The paint job still needed attention, as evidenced by the extensive amount of primer coating parts of the bodywork. The driver's door was all primer, as was the boot lid. The bonnet carried smears that made it seem like a bad attempt at camouflage. Diagonal streaks adorned the passenger door, and the roof looked as if someone had been playing noughts and crosses on it but had forgotten how to draw the grid.

But Captain Milton Garner, USAF, dressed casually in T-shirt and jeans, didn't care how the car looked from the outside. The Cobra engine he'd lovingly worked on grumbled with latent power, hinting at the massive surge on tap, should he need it. The upholstery also left much to be desired but that, too, would eventually be taken care of.

He'd been working on the car in his spare

time for nearly three years now, ever since he'd spotted it neglected and forlorn, in a corner at the back of a used-car lot in Atlanta. He could not believe, when he first saw it, that anyone could have given the Boss 429 Mustang such shabby treatment. It was the Boss of all the Boss models as far as he was concerned, and its erstwhile owner had either gone broke or was just too rich to care and had at the time seen the Mustang as just a fashionable set of wheels.

The astonished salesman had been so shocked that Garner was actually serious about buying the dilapidated car and was so pleased to be simply rid of it that he'd almost forgotten himself and nearly paid him to take it away. But the god of commerce had intervened and had soon brought him back to his senses. Even so, in the end Garner had got it for little more than the price for scrap.

It brought down the tone of his place, the salesman had said with evident relief, waving expansively at the gleaming, nearly new cars parked neatly on display. He had even offered to have the sorry Mustang transported to Garner's home.

Garner had thought the man wouldn't have

known a good car if it ran him over, but had accepted the offer.

For his part, the salesman had clearly thought Garner had taken complete leave of his senses, but was quite happy to sell a sucker a non-runner. On his wedding anniversary, he bought his mistress a present with Garner's money, while trying to persuade his wife that pressure of work had made him think of the wrong date.

When Garner eventually got the car home, he discovered that perhaps the original owner was not such a fool, after all. Though the Mustang did not have the triple-scoop Shelby bonnet and restyled nose, it had all the special equipment. He then realized that the previous owner must have once loved the car to have acquired such a special model and wondered what had dragged it to such a low station. Then the real work began.

Every leave he got, Garner worked on that car. But eventually all the hard graft and the substantial amount of money inevitably spent, paid off. This was the very first time he'd actually got it licensed and on the road once more, since its sad days with the used-car firm.

He listened in air-conditioned splendour to a track of *Mainstreet* by Bob Seger on the expensive CD system he'd installed, and enjoyed a great sense of achievement as the open road stretched before him.

He patted the steering wheel affectionately. 'That's my baby. Eat up the miles.'

He glanced in his mirror and frowned. A speck had appeared there. He was no longer alone. He was still some fifty miles from the base, and wondered if this was someone else heading for the same destination.

The bright-red, fat-wheeled, high-sitting pick-up truck roared in pursuit of the Mustang. The truck, a '96 Dodge Ram with extended cab and a heavily modified 5.2-litre V8 engine, was driven by a pig-faced man of about twenty-five who had a fixed, humourless grin stamped upon his mean features. His mean little eyes stared into the distance, malevolence seeping out of their opaque depths.

His companions, about the same age, were also male. Two of them were just as nasty-looking, with expressions of ugly anticipation on their faces. Their shirt sleeves were rolled tightly up their thick arms, almost to their shoulders.

The driver's third companion, sitting alone in the back, looked slightly younger, and was not at all happy with the situation. All four had brought pump-action shotguns.

'Look,' the unhappy one began. 'I thought we were going after rattlers. That's why I said I'd come.'

'What's the matter, boy?' the driver said disparagingly. 'This is much better than blowing the heads off rattlesnakes. You 'fraid your pappy's gonna find out?'

'Why worry, Billy?' another of the men said with a laugh. 'Hell. It's good to have a pappy who's the local sheriff.'

They all laughed, except Billy.

'Hell, Billy,' the driver was saying, 'my pappy and your pappy did this all the time when they was our age. They crossed into other states, looking for this kind of sport. You think your old man's changed that much, just because he's the sheriff?'

'Hell, no!' the three all said together, laughing raucously.

Billy looked even more unhappy.

Garner watched the speck in his mirror continue to grow, its trail of rising dust betraying its fearsome speed. He turned off the music and lowered the windows. The desert heat rolled in. After the incredible winter that had seen even Florida shivering, April in the Arizona vastness was nowhere as baking as June could be, but the temperature was high enough to get the air-conditioning working itself up furiously in an attempt to compensate. He turned it off. The warmth with the windows down and the slipstreamed breeze entering the car was quite pleasant at this time of day.

'Someone in a real hurry,' he said to himself.

He did not increase speed. There was plenty of time before he was due at the base. With the windows down, he savoured the deep growl of the cruising Cobra engine.

'And all my own work too,' he added with satisfaction.

Though he'd used the main highways on the long east-west cross-country trip, he'd deliberately begun using the back roads once he'd crossed out of Texas and into New Mexico, so as to better enjoy from time to time, with the windows down, the wonderful burble of that engine against the emptiness all around him. Only the powerful roar of the F-15 Eagle on full afterburner at take-off got to him as much.

A nighthawk, one of the whippoorwill family that confusingly liked to hunt during the day, fluttered off the side of the road as the Mustang passed, darting skywards and performing a neat barrel roll as it went.

Garner felt a slight annoyance that someone else had encroached on his solitude, but consoled himself with the fact that, given the speed the other vehicle was doing, it would soon be gone and he'd be alone again.

He thought whoever was driving was taking a chance. This was not Montana, way up north on the Canadian border, where speed limits on the open road had recently been abolished. Even in this apparently featureless place the highway patrol had a nasty habit of materializing, as if out of nowhere. He knew of at least one pilot who'd been clocked doing 140mph in a Viper on another lonely and totally empty road, by a motorcycle patrolman who'd been hiding behind a boulder. The cop had issued the ticket with a huge grin. They loved catching fast-jet aircrew.

'You're on the ground now,' the patrolman had said to the hapless pilot gleefully. 'My territory. Have a nice day.'

There was no record of what the pilot had remarked, if anything, but Garner could imagine the fury of that jet jockey's thoughts.

He glanced again at the growing speck. 'It's your licence, buddy,' he said aloud.

*   *   *

The vast airbase was many things, among which were: training unit, operational conversion unit, operational unit and, occasionally, specialist operational unit. All these identities existed concurrently within the whole and tucked away in a far corner, some distance from prying eyes, were four brand-new McDonnell-Douglas F-15 Eagles whose presence involved that specialist role.

These formidably capable two-seat aircraft could turn and fight as lethally as the single-seat version; but their real territory was in the strike arena, where they could deliver an astonishingly varied selection of weaponry, day or night, in all weathers.

But this was not their reason for being there.

'Give me an E!' Hands came together. Clap.
   'Give me an E!' came the chorus. Clap-clap.
   'Give me an A!' Clap.
   'Give me an A!' Clap-clap.
   'Give me a G!' Clap.
   'Give me a G!' Clap-clap.
   'Give me an L!' Clap.
   'Give me an L!' Clap-clap.
   'And give me an E!' Clap.
   'And give me an E!' Clap-clap.

'And give me *another* E!' Clap.

'And give me *another* E!' Clap-clap.

'We are the Eagle *Ego* drivers!' they all chorused.

The four men who made up two of the Eagle E crews were in the officers' club, 'singing' their litany in loud homage to their much-loved aircraft.

They were being observed, with barely concealed disgust, by two F-16 pilots.

'You guys are dicks,' one of them said. 'You know that?'

'Yeah,' an unrepentant back-seat occupier retorted. 'Don't you wish you had one?'

The pilot who had spoken bristled.

Doug Herlihy, a captain and one of the Eagle E pilots, sensing possible trouble, cut in quickly.

'Hey now, ladies!' he began lightly. 'Let's not forget we're all officers and gentlemen.' He had the crisp, staccato accents of a Boston patrician.

'Could have fooled me,' the F-16 pilot grumbled. 'We'll see how well you do upstairs.'

'A *challenge*?' the second back-seat man, Hal 'Computer' Mossman, remarked with fake awe. 'I *like* challenges.'

'Your itsy-bitsy toy against *ours*?' the cheerleader, a Californian named Lancer, asked in mock dismay. He clutched at his chest. 'Oh no! I'm terrified!' Lancer was a first lieutenant, and also a pilot. 'You'll give my poor lil' ol' wizzo heart failure!' He turned to the weapons systems officer who normally occupied the back seat of his aircraft. 'Say you're afraid, Johnny, boy.'

'I'm afraid, I'm afraid!' Johnny Hershon said dutifully. 'I'm really terrified.' It was Hershon who had cast doubt upon their anatomical endowment. He didn't look terrified.

'There you go,' Lancer, seeming almost too tall to get into any fighter cockpit, said to the F-16 pilot. 'We're all afraid.'

'You guys won't think it's so funny when you come up against us,' the F-16 jockey grated. 'C'mon, Norm,' he added to his companion. 'Let's leave these jokers to their fantasies.'

'"Norm",' Lancer mouthed to Hershon with a straight face. 'Aren't you pretty, Norm!' he said aloud, watching them leave the room. 'Fantasies?' he went on with a soft snarl. 'We'll show you fantasies!'

'Perhaps we shouldn't needle them,' Mossman suggested lightly. 'They're tender souls.'

'I like them needled,' Lancer retorted. 'Perhaps they'll fight better.' He turned once more to Hershon. 'You reckon these guys're Tactical

Adversary jocks? Or just regular F-16 drivers talking big?'

Among the Adversary force on the base – aircraft and pilots playing the part of the enemy during mock air combat – were many F-16 Falcons.

'Who knows?' Hershon replied. 'They're not wearing any Adversary badges that I could see.'

'Who cares?' Mossman said. 'We'll still whup 'em, but good.'

They laughed.

Just then another Eagle pilot turned up. Captain Matt Sukowinsky came from New York and sounded like it.

'Anyone heard from the Jazz Couple?' he asked. 'It's getting close to briefing time.'

'You worry too much, Sukowinsky,' Moss-man said. He was Sukowinsky's WSO. 'It's two and a half hours yet. Have a coffee and sit down.'

'What's the Jazz Couple?' Lancer asked.

Sukowinsky gave him a jaded look. 'I keep forgetting you're our new tenderfoot, plucked fresh from the selfish Eagles.' It was his way of describing the pilot-only, single-seat versions of the aircraft. 'Captains Nathan "The Ball" Adderly, and Milton "The Sax" Garner. We call them the Jazz Couple because they've got the names of two of the greatest jazzmen that ever lived: Cannonball Adderley, and Errol Garner. Sometimes, we also call them Nate and Milt. You should wait till you know them better before doing that.'

It was a testament to Lancer's and Hershon's success as a crew that they had made it into the special unit while Garner and Adderly had been away.

'They're related to these guys?' Lancer asked.

'No,' Herlihy began patiently. 'They're just namesakes. The Jazz Couple also hate each other's guts.'

Lancer stared at him. 'You're kidding. And the Air Force put them in the *same* plane?'

'Ah well, you see,' Herlihy told him, 'they're like a married couple. Can't live with each other, but can't live without each other. In short, they chew all comers in the air. Whatever it is we're here for, they're the ones to beat.'

'We can beat them. Can't we, Johnny?'

'Sure,' Hershon replied, not looking as if he believed it.

'What I like,' Sukowinsky said, favouring Lancer with a sceptical stare, 'is confidence in the air. In your dreams, buddy. You're not in single-seaters any more. This is a whole new ball game, as you should've learned by now.'

'We'll see.' But Lancer's curiosity was aroused. 'Why do they hate each other?'

Silence greeted the question.

'Aw c'mon,' Lancer persisted. 'If it's such a big secret, why tell me about them in the first place?'

'You'd have noticed sooner or later, I guess,' Sukowinsky remarked with mild resignation.

'So . . . tell me the rest.'

Herlihy decided to do the telling; but he uttered the sigh of a man who had travelled too far and dreaded continuing.

'By some bizarre twist of fate, as they say,' he began, taking over from Sukowinsky, 'Sax Garner discovered that Adderly's family once owned slaves, Garner's ancestors among them.'

'You've got to be kidding.'

'As someone whose own forebears sailed with the Pilgrims to escape the King's minions, I don't kid about such things. Adderly's people really did own slaves, and those out of whose loins sprang the modern-day Garners were indeed among them. According to the documents, the Adderlys were not the nicest of the Southern slave owners. In fact, if they gave Oscars for being bastards, then the slaver Adderlys would have won every time. Today's supremacists would love them.'

Fascinated, Lancer stared at him. 'So now the Adderlys are rich white folk and the Garners are poor black? That's why Garner still hates them?'

Someone gave a chuckle.

'I said something funny?'

'Got it all wrong, tenderfoot,' Mossman said. 'Garner hates them all right. From what we've heard, they did some terrible things to his kinfolk, even by slave-owner standards. But the Garners are *rich* black folk and the Adderlys, for their sins, while not down there in the dirt, are the *poor* white folk by comparison. Seems sometime in the last century the market went out of slavery,' he added, straight-faced.

'You're kidding,' Lancer said for the third time.

'He likes using those words, doesn't he?' Sukowinsky murmured.

Lancer ignored his remark and looked to Hershon for help. Hershon shrugged.

'You could almost say,' Mossman went on, 'under different circumstances, Adderly could easily have been Garner's chauffeur . . .'

'Which of course,' Herlihy began mildly, 'is

what he really is.' He smiled at Lancer. 'If you get my meaning.'

'I get it. You guys are having some fun with me. Well, thank you for nothing.'

Sukowinsky shook his head solemnly. 'It is true about the slaves, and Garner really is rich – kind of. Word is, his father's a financial wizard. The old man was in financial circles when a black face in that line of business was scarcer than snow on a hot day. Moved to New York from the South, but they've still got family and a home down there. He bought one of those Southern mansions that had been a wreck for years, and built it right up again. Some kind of historical justice, huh?'

'The Adderlys' home?'

'No, Lieutenant Lancer. *That* would be too much coincidence.'

'Talking of wrecks,' Herlihy said. 'Didn't Garner say he'd finished that wreck he's been working on for nearly three years? That Mustang no one's ever seen.'

'Like father like son,' Sukowinsky commented drily. 'If he is driving that thing, he probably won't get here at all.'

'We don't even know for sure he's a . . .' Billy began, then stopped.

'C'mon, Billy!' the driver of the pick-up urged. 'Say it, say it!' he encouraged, as if at some initiation. 'Goddamit! Are you your daddy's boy, or some peckerwood? He and my pappy had some rare ol' times across in Alabama and Georgia way back in the sixties. "Nigger weekends" they used to call it, my pappy said.'

'We don't know he's . . . black.'

'That's not the word, Billy,' the driver said coldly.

'Oh leave me be, Amos!'

'Leave him be, he says. Goddamit, Billy! Nigger's the word. *Nigger!*'

The other men giggled slyly.

'Didn't you see that car go by just before we came to that corner just out of town? The way it looked? Hell, it wasn't even painted. That was a nigger car for sure. No pride in anything, niggers. Give 'em welfare every week. That's all they want.'

'I got a bad feeling about this, Amos.'

Amos turned to look at the younger man. 'Don't you go cissy on me, Billy.'

'Jesus!' one of the men yelled. 'Watch the damn road, Amos!'

The pick-up had veered alarmingly.

'Hold on to your balls, Yannock. I was

driving pick-ups since I was a tick in my daddy's porker. Don't you tell me how to drive this damn thing.'

Garner was again checking his mirrors. The speck had metamorphosed into a red pick-up truck. It came on without slackening pace. It would soon catch up and pass him, he reasoned. Then he'd be all alone once more to enjoy the vastness about him.

After several moments had gone by and the truck made no move to pull out to overtake, Garner began to wonder what the other driver was up to, and felt a strange tension rise within him. Perhaps it was nothing. He was just being jumpy, he persuaded himself. The otherwise empty road was suddenly spooking him. There was nothing to worry about.

But the truck was almost filling the mirrors, and it made no move to overtake.

Garner kept his nerve and did not accelerate. 'Pass, damn you!' he hissed.

The truck stayed put. Then it began to get closer still. Soon its image had spilled out beyond the edges of the mirrors.

It was now nearly crawling up the back of the Mustang.

'Wha'd I tell you?' Amos crowed. 'A nigger!'

Suddenly he pulled out and matched speeds with the Mustang. He began to blow the loud air-horns.

The two vehicles travelled side by side for a while.

Garner glanced across and saw the men grinning down at him from the high cab, and felt a weary resignation.

He'd travelled right across the country without the slightest problem of this kind, and this was the last place he'd expected it. But that particular boil was still so deep within the guts of the nation it leaked its poison anywhere, and any time. This bunch of retards had decided he was their sport for the day.

But he should have expected it, he told himself angrily. There were all sorts of gun-happy white supremacists inhabiting the desert backcountry. He should have known.

The occupants of the pick-up were yelling and whooping. He couldn't see the person in the back properly, but he didn't appear to be joining in the fun.

'Hey, boy!' one of them yelled from the cab. 'That's some car you got there! What's the matter? The pimping business not going too good? Not enough welfare?'

The truck had now come so close that if they

had stopped, neither door on the opposing sides would have opened fully.

Garner gave Yannock a cold glance.

'Hey! See that? He's got grey eyes! You've got grey eyes, boy! There's a lil' bit of white in you! Some nice white man porked your mammy, boy?' Yannock gave him an ugly grin, deliberately goading. 'An' don't give me one of them looks. I'd just as soon blow your damn fool head to kingdom come, right here!'

This, Garner decided, could get seriously dangerous. It was time for some discretion over valour.

He changed down a gear and stamped on the accelerator.

The Mustang squealed its rear wheels and suddenly rocketed away, a powerful roar echoing in its wake. The pick-up rapidly became a pinprick once more.

'Sweet Jesus!' Yannock exclaimed, gaping. 'What the hell has he got under that hood?'

'I don't like this,' Billy said from the back.

'*Shut up!*' Amos snarled at him, humiliated by the Mustang's easy escape. He floored the accelerator. Though the pick-up took off with alacrity, even its modified engine was no real match for the Mustang. But he kept going, driving at the edge of control. 'No nigger's gonna make a fool out of me, *goddamit*!' He thumped the steering wheel twice.

Amos had become what those stupid enough to be his friends called 'killing mean'.

The red Dodge pick-up raced after the fleeing Mustang.

Some distance away, Deputy Sheriff Zack Milson focused his powerful binoculars on a fast-moving shape that had come round a wide bend in the road, and into view. He was standing on an escarpment, looking down on the otherwise empty black ribbon that fed its way across the parched landscape.

'Got us a race driver here, Sheriff!' he called eagerly to his superior. 'Must be doing a hundred, at least. Maybe more.'

He stepped back slightly to look behind him. About fifty feet down at the bottom of a gentle, shale and rock-strewn slope, the patrol car was hidden behind one of those tall rock sculptures that had graced many a Western.

The sheriff, a grey-haired, thickset man, had removed his hat and was dabbing at his forehead with a handkerchief. He was leaning against the car.

'How long before he gets close enough?'

Sheriff Jess Newberg, Billy's father, called up.

'We got some time.' Milson was once more focusing on the road. He tracked the binoculars rearwards from the speeding Mustang. 'Hey! What the hell's this?'

Newberg put his hat back on. 'You tell me, Zack,' he said wearily. 'You're the one looking.'

'There's another car . . . no it's a pick-up . . . and it's racing too. Those nuts are having a race, Sheriff!'

'Well now . . . we'll just have to spoil their fun.'

'Hell, Sheriff,' Milson continued, the binoculars clamped to his eyes. 'I know that pick-up. It's Amos Brant's.'

'Goddam that idiot!' the sheriff growled. 'Probably got his idiot friends with him too.'

Milson was hurrying down. 'He's not gonna catch that Mustang. That thing's *moving*. It'll be hitting the county line soon.'

Newberg eased himself off the car. 'How far are *we* from the county line, Zack?'

Milson reacted by glancing involuntarily to his left. A few yards away a sign informed travellers they were leaving the county.

'Well come *on*, Zack. Get into the car and

put it across the road. Our fast man in the Mustang's going nowhere before we've had a little talk with him.'

'Yes, sir!' Milson hurriedly got into the patrol car.

'And get those lights moving. Better bring out one of the shotguns too.'

'Yes, sir!' Milson repeated, started the car and lurched towards the road to place the vehicle broadside on, straddling the centreline. The roof lights began to flash.

Milson grabbed one of the shotguns, and quickly climbed out. Feet planted apart, he positioned himself at the ready near the patrol car, as Newberg joined him.

They waited, looking down the road in the direction from which the Mustang and the pick-up would be coming.

Newberg did not draw his own sidearm.

'Shit!' Garner exclaimed softly as he saw the lights of the police car. 'I don't need this.'

He began to slow down.

'He's slowing down!' Yannock chortled. 'He's busted his goddam engine! We got you now, niggerboy!' Then he saw the lights. 'Oh hell!' he added.

'I knew it!' Billy Newberg said. 'Goddamit, Amos!'

'*Shut the fuck up, Billy!*' Brant snarled. 'You hear me?'

'Well, well,' the sheriff said to his deputy as the Mustang came towards them at a crawl, then stopped. 'What have we here. Georgia plates and a nigger at the wheel. You cover me, Zack. I'm gonna have me a talk with the fast nigger.'

'You got it, Sheriff,' Milson acknowledged with a smirk, bringing the shotgun up but staying by the car.

The sheriff walked stiff-legged towards the Mustang.

The pick-up had slowed down and had also stopped, some distance behind.

'Damn!' Billy cried. 'It's my father! Turn this thing round, Amos!'

'You think he's blind? He's already seen us. Relax. Your daddy doesn't like niggers any more than we do. He'll take him in, and we can have him later. Let's watch this.'

Garner watched neutrally as the sheriff stopped a short distance away.

'Out of the car, boy!' Newberg ordered, and

placed a precautionary hand on the gun at his hip.

Garner complied expressionlessly.

'What's a Georgia boy doing way out here, racing on the public highway?' Newberg demanded.

'I wasn't racing,' Garner replied calmly. 'Those morons in that pick-up tried to run me off the road. They're looking for trouble. I was just getting away from them.'

Newberg didn't like the way Garner had responded. His face clouded over.

'Let's hear some respect in your voice, boy, when you talk to me. *Hands on the car!* You know the drill. And no funny moves. My deputy back there's got a nervous disposition. The last time he got nervous he blew some guy's face clean off with that pump gun. Now I'm gonna search you for weapons . . .'

'I think you should see my ID, Sheriff, before this gets worse . . .'

'Don't interrupt me, boy! You hear what I'm saying?'

'I hear you.'

'And you talk funny for a black Georgia boy. You sound like a Yankee.'

'My family moved to New York,' Garner told him, still keeping calm. 'But we've got a home in

27

Georgia.' Jumpy backcountry sheriffs and their deputies tended to have 'accidents'. He wasn't keen to add to the number. 'Please check my ID, Sheriff. Holding me here is against the national interest, as you will soon see.'

Newberg paused. 'You telling me you're one of them fancy black FBI agents?' he began sceptically, an unpleasant grin on his face. 'You know . . . fancy-talking college boys – like you sound – in sharp suits. Only you got no sharp suit on. You one of them?' The sneer in his voice fairly leapt at Garner.

'No, Sheriff.'

There was another pause.

'Well, then,' Newberg drawled. 'Better let me see that ID you're so all fired up about.' He was clearly having fun, and did not believe Garner. 'And if you're messing with me, you're going to be one sorry black boy. You got that? You'll wish that pick-up had run you off the road. No funny moves now. Remember my nervous deputy.'

Garner slowly reached into his jeans for his USAF ID, then handed it to Newberg.

There was a long silence as Newberg studied it.

'No shit.' Another silence followed. 'Captain Garner,' Newberg continued at last to himself.

'Yeah, yeah.' He glanced up at the sky, and sighed. He looked as if he wanted to spit. 'United States Air Force. Straighten up, Captain.' He spat on to the edge of the road.

Garner obeyed, and turned round.

Newberg handed back the ID, then cleared his throat. It was obvious he hated what he was going to have to say.

'Uh, look. Sorry, Captain . . . I . . .'

'Forget it, Sheriff,' Garner interrupted coolly. With all the bases in the area, he'd expected that even a local sheriff would have been less quick to jump to the wrong conclusions. But prejudice was like that. 'We all make mistakes,' he added.

He got back into the Mustang and started the engine. It burst into powerful life and grumbled at idle. 'I'm expected at my base soon,' he continued. 'Got to get going. Could you please ask your man to move the patrol car?'

Newberg's eyes danced briefly. He gnawed at his lower lip, hating even more the fact that he was forced to do Garner's bidding.

'Sure. *Zack!*'

He didn't turn to look at his deputy. His eyes continued to stare at Garner, as if in thrall.

'Sheriff?'

'Move the car! We don't want to delay the Captain . . .'

'*Captain* . . .'

'Goddamit, Zack. Get the damn car out of the way!'

'Yessir, Sheriff!'

Milson hurried back into the patrol car to carry out his superior's orders.

As the patrol car lurched out of the way, Garner eased the Mustang slowly forward.

'Thank you, Sheriff.' Garner gave Newberg a casual salute.

Involuntarily, Newberg responded before he realized what he was doing. He brought his hand back down guiltily, and turned to watch as the Mustang roared across the county line.

'*Shit, shit, shit!*' Yannock fumed. 'I don't get it. He's let him go! What the hell do you make of that?'

Amos Brant gripped at the wheel and said nothing.

'Perhaps he was police,' Billy suggested. 'He gave my father something. Must've been an ID. My father even saluted him. You all saw.'

'Now I've seen it all,' Yannock said. 'Sheriff Newberg, terror of the niggers, salutin' one. That sure beats all.'

'*Are you two assholes going to stop yam-mering?*' Amos Brant yelled.

By the police car, Newberg was still star-ing after the rapidly receding Mustang. He looked like a man who'd been cheated, and he wanted to vent his frustration on something, or someone.

'Get on the speakers, Zack,' he said at last to his deputy, 'and get those peckerheads in that pick-up down here.'

'I think your son's with them, Sheriff,' Milson announced tentatively. 'I've been watching the truck . . .'

'Goddamit, Zack! Quit arguin' with me! I don't give a shit if the President himself's in that truck. You think I'm going up to them and say please? *Get them here!*'

'Yes, sir!' Zack acknowledged quickly, and turned on the patrol car's loudspeakers to order the pick-up to approach.

When the Dodge had arrived Newberg glared at the occupants, reserving the hardest look for his son.

'Amos Brant,' he began formally, 'I'm arrest-ing you for speeding on the public highway . . .'

Brant refused to believe it at first. 'C'mon, Uncle Jess. It was just a bit of fun . . .'

Newberg shut him up with a baleful stare. 'You're going to lose that licence, Amos.'

Brant was scandalized. 'You can't . . .'

'I can, and I will. I'm the sheriff. Remember?'

'But Uncle Jess . . . I drive a truck for a living. What am I gonna do without my licence?'

'Should've thought about that, boy, before you decided to go on a coon hunt. Now come on out. Get into the car with Zack. C'mon. *Move!*'

Brant climbed reluctantly out, still wanting to believe that Newberg would only go so far. But it was the wrong day for favours.

Newberg's eyes searched out his son. 'Billy!' There was no warmth in them.

'Yes, sir!'

'You get behind that wheel and drive the pick-up back to town. Go on.'

'Yes . . . yes, sir!'

2

Garner did not enjoy the remainder of the journey to the base. The incident with the pick-up and the sheriff had soured the pleasure the long drive had given him. Worse, it had reminded him of his continuing antipathy for his pilot.

As a man and an officer in the United States Air Force, he felt secure within himself. As an American, he felt secure in his rights as a citizen. As a black American, he felt the burden of his nation's history weighing heavily upon him. As one of the crew pair of his F-15 Eagle E, for him that burden had become sharply focused.

The aircraft, he felt, symbolized all the contradictions of the powerful country that had become the United States; but like the aircraft, there was an almost omnipotent capability, accompanied by an unmistakable tension. The potential of this tension for disaster – which was on all the streets of the nation – could only be guessed at, and was thus to be much feared. There was the constant awareness that the glue that held the country together could come unstuck at any moment.

Garner loved his country, and loved his profession. It was a calling. Clinically, he knew that Adderly was an excellent pilot. He knew they worked well together, as long as he did not allow his own personal feelings to surface while in the air. On the ground, it was another matter altogether; but in the interests of discipline, he kept that in check. However, there was still a discernible tension between pilot and back-seater, when they were not flying. They kept their social contact within strict limits.

Not for the first time, he cursed the fate that had brought the two of them together.

Throughout the States, the descendants of slaver and enslaved crossed one another's paths every day. But how many not only personally *knew* the descendant of his family's slavers, but actually *worked* with one in the confined cockpit space of one of the world's most technically advanced combat aircraft?

Perhaps, defying the odds, there were many such; but he would always consider his own situation unique.

Half an hour later he pulled up at the wide gates to the base. A young air force policeman he did not recognize came up to the car, studying it with more than passing interest.

The policeman looked at the ID that Garner held up to him, but his eyes were really for the car.

'Yes, sir, thank you, Captain,' he said, saluting smartly. 'You've got one hell of a car there, sir,' he continued. 'A 429. Best of all the Boss Mustangs. You working on her, sir?'

Garner was impressed. He had not yet remounted the badging on the car.

'Yes. I am. You know your Mustangs,' he added to the air policeman.

The younger man grinned. 'Sure love those cars, sir. Last of the great Americans. I know Corvette crazies would hate to hear that but for me, the Mustang's the thing . . . the Boss 429 most of all. Got me a '66 convertible back home. She's not running yet but when I'm done she's gonna look like a GT350. I've already got me a four-barrel Holly carb on the 289 engine, and some big-finned wheels. She's gonna look real good, sir.'

'I'll bet.' Garner looked at the enlisted man's name tag. 'Is that a Georgia accent I'm listening to, Lyle?'

'It sure is, sir. Mason Lyle, from Macon, GA, like in the song.'

'That was Philadelphia, PA.'

Lyle grinned. 'Nobody comes from Philadelphia.'

'Except Philadelphians.'

'Like I said, nobody.'

'Well, don't let any Phillies on this base hear you,' Garner advised the smiling air policeman. 'I'm a Georgia man, born, but bred elsewhere,' he continued. 'My folks come from just outside Olympic City.'

'Atlanta, huh?'

'Queen of the South, herself. Spent my youth in New York, so the accent's taken a beating.'

'They can take the man out of the South, sir, but they sure can't take the South out of the man.'

'Amen to that, Lyle,' Garner agreed, for many reasons, as he prepared to drive off.

'Excuse me, sir.'

Garner paused.

'I was thinking, sir,' Lyle continued, 'if you'd like some help with the car I'd . . . well . . . I'd like to offer . . . I'm pretty good, sir.'

Garner smiled at him. 'I might just take you up on that.'

'Sir, thank you, sir!'

Lyle saluted once more as Garner drove on.

Their friendly talk went some way towards removing some of the sourness from the day after the encounter with the hick sheriff and the men in the pick-up.

There it was again, he thought wryly: the contradictions inherent within the nation. Lyle was pure Georgia and probably even came from a family that had made life hell for the blacks during the sixties. Yet Lyle, despite the fact that Garner was an Eagle crewman and an officer, still looked upon the captain simply as a fellow Georgian; a compatriot with whom a bond had been formed, sharing the love of the classic Mustang.

Garner felt appreciably better.

Colonel Robert E. Dempsey, a Texan, had a voice which, even when used softly, tended to fill the space about him irrespective, it sometimes appeared, of the size of the room he happened to be in at the time. However, for anyone seeing him for the first time the truly remarkable thing about him was his stature. For Dempsey was a small man; so small, he was frequently mistaken for a boy ... until one saw the colonel's eagles on his shoulders, or his lapels; or looked into his eyes. A tall, slim major stood next to him, vividly accentuating the difference in height.

Looking so much younger than his real age tended to cause confusion in others; but the colonel was a veteran of many combat missions, and legend had it that he could fly any aircraft with his eyes shut. Even allowing for the exaggeration, there was no doubt that he had an impressive flying history. The stack of medal ribbons beneath the pilot's wings on his left breast when he was in full uniform were more than sufficient testimony. Among other things on the base, he was responsible for bringing the special Eagle E unit up to speed, for the as-yet-unknown mission.

Dempsey, inevitably nicknamed Robert E. Lee, stood before the assembled crews, legs parted, hands gripping his hips. His cropped, grey-flecked black hair seemed incongruous atop the baby-like features.

'Can you all see me properly?' the booming voice demanded.

'Yes, sir!' they chorused. No one would dare make a joke about his height.

'Good.' His lively blue eyes raked his audience. 'We seem to be one officer light. Where is Mr Adderly?' The eyes fastened upon Garner. 'Mr Garner . . . where's your pilot?'

'Er . . .' Garner began.

'Sir!' Someone had entered the room. Adderly came briskly to attention. 'Sorry I'm late, *sir*!'

Dempsey stared at him for long moments. 'Don't do it again, Captain,' the deep voice said quietly. It was almost as if he had pronounced sentence.

'No, sir!'

'Sit down, Mr Adderly.' Dempsey did not ask for an explanation and in a way this was a far more effective censure.

'Yes, sir!' Adderly took an empty chair next to Garner. He did not look at his back-seater.

'Now that we're all here,' Dempsey continued, without a trace of sarcasm, 'we can commence this briefing.'

They watched him intently.

'For the past six weeks,' he went on, 'your training missions have been in competition with each other. The four crews remaining are those who have, in my estimation, merited getting this far. This is not a downer on the capabilities of the crews that have not made it. They will return to their units without a stain on their confidential records. The quality of all those who made it for this contest was commendably high.'

Dempsey briefly scratched the tip of his nose with a little finger. Those who knew him well understood this to be a signal that he had a small bomb to drop somewhere along the line, always unexpectedly.

'The mission for which you are being tested will require an exceptional team in the cockpit. This crew will carry out the mission, with one more as a back-up should, for any reason, whoever has made the top spot be unable to continue. I know Eagles like to prowl in pairs, but this is a very special mission. It requires just the one ship.

'The winning Echo Eagle's pilot and wizzo will be told the mission on the day of take-off for the forward base. The back-up will not be informed, unless it becomes necessary to carry out the mission in place of that first airplane. From today, we go into a new phase. If you thought things were tough before, think again. This is crunch time. Each crew will fly two hops today. One this afternoon and one tonight. On each of these flights you will be bounced at any time, by the Tactical Adversary Falcons. How you cope will decide your eventual position at the finish.

'Oh yes, gentlemen,' Dempsey added, as if the thought had just come to him. The bomb was coming. 'I'll be flying one of the Falcons. You won't know which, so stay alert. If you find me crawling all over your six, God help you.'

There were subdued groans at this.

Dempsey looked at his crews and didn't smile. 'Take over, Major Carter.'

'Sir,' the major acknowledged. 'Right, gentlemen,' he went on as Dempsey left. 'You know what's expected of you. Weather for today is perfect as usual.' He gave a wicked grin. 'Nice for us to see you by.'

'Don't tell us you're going hunting as well, sir,' Hershon pleaded.

Robert E. *and* Carter. Crapville.

Carter's smile was feral. 'It's bad news day, Hershon.' Carter was known as 'Killer'; with good reason.

'This is just great,' Lancer began after Carter had followed Dempsey. 'Just great. Old Robert E. Lee himself *and* the nasty neighbourhood major, playing at bogeys. Dempsey hates staying on the ground, and as for Carter, he *enjoys* taking out Eagle jocks. The man's a sadist. They'll cream *all* our asses.'

'Worse,' Hershon joined in, 'we won't know if we're tangling with one of those Falcon jocks we saw in the club, or the old man himself, or Carter. Until it's way too late.'

'If Robert E. decides to fly on all the adversary missions,' Sukowinsky began tentatively, 'he'll be tired. That might give us a chance.' There was more hope than belief in those words.

'You wish,' Mossman commented drily. 'He *never* gets tired. That guy's so fit, I feel weak just looking at him. We'll wear him out, he'll be laughing so much.'

'Well, *any* F-16 we see,' Adderly said, 'I'm going to assume it's him, or Carter, and act accordingly. Better safe.'

Garner nodded. 'I agree. They're both going to be out to get us. It's the mean season, guys.' He turned to his pilot. 'We'd better get suited up. We've got the first hop.'

Adderly nodded. 'Yeah. Just our luck.'

'I'll pray for you turkeys,' Lancer called after them as they left the room together. 'Robert E. Lee will be good and fresh, and just hungry for suckers! And if he doesn't get you, the sadist will!' He gave a loud and passable imitation of the gobbling sound of the hapless bird in a blind panic. 'And if they don't, *we* will in the fly-off.'

Lancer clearly believed his aircraft would be in the last two to survive the predations of the colonel and the major.

'Pray for yourselves!' Garner retorted. 'You'll need it more than us.'

Lancer's laughter followed them out.

'We're going to have to teach that guy a lesson he'll never forget,' Garner went on to Adderly. 'He thinks he can beat us.'

'That'll be the day,' Adderly said.

They walked on in silence for a while, then Garner said, 'What happened?'

'Why was I late?'

Garner nodded.

'Small problem at home. I missed the earlier flight back.' Adderly did not elaborate.

Garner did not press the issue, but he knew it was more than a 'small' problem. He knew what had caused Adderly to be late for the start of the briefing.

Adderly was married, with a baby boy. It was not his first child. The earlier one, a girl, had died during birth, nearly killing her mother as well. Arlene Adderly, previously a sparkling, outgoing person, had become very introverted after that. When Garner and Adderly had been sent on temporary assignment from their base in North Carolina to Arizona, she had been very unhappy. The new baby had just arrived. Adderly could have cited the situation and requested removal from the assignment; but his commitment to his career was such that he would never have contemplated making such a request.

Garner also knew that a now very much changed Arlene would like her husband to leave the air force, though she would never admit this publicly, even in her current state. But flying fast jets was all that Adderly knew, and all that he wanted to do. To take him away would be like depriving him of a great part of his life. He would not be the same man she had fallen in love with, and subsequently married. But for the moment, she was not the woman he'd married either.

Though not married himself, Garner could well sympathize with Adderly's situation. His own dreams of marriage had foundered upon the rocks of a disastrous love affair. The woman in question had been someone from his school days. He'd fallen for her from the first day he'd seen her at school. Then her family had moved to California and they'd lost touch for years. But he'd never forgotten her.

One day, during vacation with his family to celebrate his brand-new commission, he'd unexpectedly bumped into her – literally – in a New York department store.

Then a budding financial whiz-kid, she'd

joined a New York firm. They continued where they'd left off, as if the years had not intervened. The affair was intense, but something was wrong. The years *had* changed things. An officer in the air force was small beer, and a husband with a military career was not high on her list of priorities. She would never become an air force flyer's wife, she'd told him bluntly. Airline, maybe. Why hadn't he gone into finance, like his father? But despite this personal downgrading, he'd still felt a powerful physical attraction to her. She'd reciprocated with an almost consuming enthusiasm.

Garner had hung on to that dream for two years; but the damage had long been done. One weekend he arrived in New York from his North Carolina base to spend the time with her. That first night they had a romantic dinner in a fashionable restaurant, followed by long bouts of ferocious lovemaking in her apartment, for the remainder of the weekend. She'd dropped the bombshell on the morning of his last day in town. She was going to marry someone from Wall Street.

Benumbed, he'd walked out and checked into a hotel, waiting out the time before his return flight by making a close acquaintance with a bottle of bourbon. He'd found it hard to equate the person who'd had the dinner with him, who had made such fantastic love during the weekend, with the one who had acted with such clinical ruthlessness. The condemned man had eaten a hearty dinner, enjoyed hearty, wild sex, and eaten a hearty breakfast. Then dropped through the trapdoor.

Astonishingly, he'd made it back to his quarters on the base without disgracing himself. But that night the pain of the loss hit him with a vengeance and he'd vomited until there was nothing left to bring up. The bourbon had not been solely responsible.

He didn't see her again.

To compensate, he concentrated single-mindedly on his job and became an even better wizzo than he already was. For recreation, he spent most of his spare time visiting relatives in Georgia, and working on the Mustang. That way, he'd managed to keep her out of his mind. She sent letters, asking him to be happy for her. Driven by guilt, he'd reasoned coldly. He'd ripped the letters to shreds, and never replied. Eventually they had stopped coming.

Then the air force teamed him up with Adderly.

It was during that dark period that he discovered the history of the Adderly family and, as with so many things in life, it had occurred innocuously. Adderly had introduced him to Arlene, herself a Southern beauty from Arkansas. One evening, during a dinner at the Adderlys' home near the base, he and Arlene had found themselves alone and she'd said something quite casually, never dreaming of the repercussions.

'It's kinda great,' she'd said, 'the air force putting you and Nate together in the same plane. Who'd have thought that before the Civil War, Nate's family owned slaves who were part of your family?'

Stunned by the revelation, he'd made no big deal about it at the time, keeping his true reactions to himself.

'How do you know that?' he'd asked her as calmly as he could.

Quite unaware of the effect the news had had on him, she'd replied easily, 'Oh, Nate's got some of the family papers among his junk. He told me.'

'He never told me.'

'Well, he wouldn't, would he? He's kinda embarrassed about that part of the family history. But just before the Civil War, the last Adderly to inherit the plantation freed all the slaves. *He* was against slavery. Nate reckons that's when the family started to get poor. He's proud about that.'

'I guess.'

Garner never forgave Adderly for not telling him and decided to do some investigation of his own. Perhaps if the woman he'd loved so deeply had not dumped him, he would not have channelled his pain into finding out about the Adderlys and their slaves. From his own family, he'd known of the slave history, but no one had ever told him of the Adderly connection, even when he'd introduced his then new pilot. The reason had been simple enough. The existence of the branch of the Garner family who'd been Adderly slaves had been unknown.

Garner had started dividing his spare time between the trips to Georgia to work on the Mustang, and digging into the past. During his researches, he discovered a personal journal in an obscure library in West Virginia, of all places. How it had got there from Georgia was anyone's guess. No one at the library had seemed to know. The book itself was of little importance to them. They'd looked upon it as just another account among the countless number of written words about slavery.

The Journal of Nathan Adderly, had been

written on the soft, faded cover, in neat copperplate. It was dated 1837.

That particular Nathan Adderly had been the last of the real slave owners of the family, before Josiah Adderly had turned everything on its head and freed the human beings he'd inherited. Nathan Adderly had also been a master of unspeakable cruelty and his thoughts had been set down in the journal, in an almost businesslike way. There was no feeling for the suffering he had caused in his fellow human beings.

Garner had found no discernible emotion in the narrative as the facts, noted down by Nathan Adderly, had screamed their horror at him.

An entry, dated and timed, had grabbed Garner's attention: 'Caught a runaway. Enoch by name. Punished him to teach others a lesson. Tied him to a tree and slit his nose. He squealed like a hog. He won't be going anywhere now.'

The matter-of-fact tone had sickened Garner and brought the sharp taste of nausea into his mouth. He'd forced himself to continue reading, scanning through the many other entries, each vying with the rest for horrific content.

By the time he'd perused Nathan Adderly's

personal record as much as he'd wanted to, he'd also discovered something even more horrific in that precise account of one man's capacity for inhumanity.

The entry in question spoke of a rape – as recorded by Nathan Adderly – by a young black male slave, of a teenage daughter of the family. She had been made pregnant as a result.

'Mercifully,' Adderly's ancestor had written, 'the wretched animal that issued out of her loins was dead at birth. She has been confined, as during the pregnancy, to keep our shame from other eyes. None, except her servant, will cast eyes upon her. She is not to be visited by any of the family. I am no longer father to this daughter. The slaves mutter among themselves, a dreadful calumny upon her. They say she was not raped! How dare these savage beasts of the fields cast such aspersions! That my daughter Helena would willingly consort with a young buck is beyond imagining! But, as I have written, she is no longer my daughter.'

Nathan Adderly had taken a terrible revenge.

He'd had the young slave, himself a teenager, eviscerated alive. And he'd written it all down, describing the terrible process in full, almost loving detail. He'd watched from beginning to end. There'd been no law to stop him and in any case, no one would have. Slaves were not human.

Garner had walked out of the genteel little library feeling soiled, and for a while had stood outside in the warmth of a bright day gulping for air as he tried to regain his emotional equilibrium. He'd looked at the faces passing by, and had wondered how many of them knew of the dark horrors confided to that faded, innocent-looking journal. Had any of them ever come upon it? And would they have cared even if they had?

Then, as now, he doubted it.

My country, my pain, he'd thought as he stood there watching the oblivious people walk past.

He'd told no one about what he'd found; not even his father who, even now, knew nothing of it. He'd also wondered whether Nathan Adderly knew anything about those particular pastimes of his nineteenth-century namesake.

For Garner, the poisoned knowledge made him hate the Adderly family even more.

But he was genuinely concerned about Arlene's health. He had nothing against her and before the miscarriage she'd always been pleasant company, humorous and sometimes quite daring.

'In certain lighting, you and Nate look alike,' she'd once said to him one warm evening, in sultry Arkansas tones laced with Louisiana and oiled by Southern Comfort. 'You know that? You got the same grey eyes too.'

Before she'd married Adderly, her name had been Labouchere. Her family had moved from Louisiana to Arkansas before she was born, but their accents had been grafted on to those of the state of her birth. The blend had given her a devastatingly sensuous voice.

'Would I know the difference in the dark?' she'd added mischievously.

'You'd better!' her husband had warned drily, coming up to them with replenished drinks. 'Behave yourself, Arlene. Quit hitting on my wizzo. I might get jealous.'

But that had been before Garner had discovered about the first Nathan Adderly. Days of innocence. Fun times.

'How's Arlene doing?' he now asked.

'She's OK,' Adderly replied, just short of being curt. 'She's going to be all right. Plenty of family to spend time with her.'

'That's good.'

They walked on in silence, to get kitted up. Fun times.

For a fighter, the standard single-seat F-15 Eagle was a huge beast. If anything, the F-15E, also known as the Echo Eagle or Eagle E, looked subtly bigger but was in fact of roughly the same dimensions. It was the conformal tanks – allowing extra fuel and thus range – tucked inboard beneath the wing on either side of the airframe, that served to give the F-15E an aggressive, broad-shouldered and awesome presence. Its vital statistics were no less awesome. Many people swore that the huge wing was as big as a tennis court. At nearly sixty-four feet long and close to eighteen and a half feet high to the tips of the vast sails of its twin fins, the aircraft was no midget.

The F-15E was not pretty in the ordinary sense of the word; but to those lucky enough to fly it, that big wing – all 608 square feet of it – made the Eagle E so agile that in the hands of a pilot who knew his stuff, few existing fighter aircraft could cope with it.

So it bounced about a bit at very low altitudes because of that playing field of a wing, and was not a smooth ride down there. So what? Garner thought. It made up for that drawback in many other ways. A dual-role aircraft, it was devastatingly effective against ground as well as air targets. It could pull more positive G than even the standard F-15 – 9 to the single-seater's 7.2 – and certainly more than its crew, even with their suits to help them, could. Even in the most violent of manoeuvring combat they couldn't break it, unless they slammed into something. It would break them first.

Many fast-jet crews would kill to get into its roomy, air-conditioned cockpits, Garner knew, and he felt highly privileged to be one of the fortunate few who'd actually made it.

As in all things, it was not without its detractors. The single-seat crews had various derogatory names for it: 'mudhen' and 'pregnant duck' were among the more polite epithets. To Garner, it was all sour grapes. Sheer jealousy.

The Echo Eagle could carry a formidable array of weaponry, from various air-to-ground munitions to three types of air-to-air missiles. For close-in work there was the internal Vulcan 20mm, six-barrelled rotary cannon. She could fly in all weathers, and her LANTIRN navigation and attack pods enabled her to find the enemy, irrespective of conditions outside. In the dark, an infrared image superimposed on the head-up display gave the crew a window on the night.

Today, Garner decided, he and Adderly were going to ruin an F-16 jock's entire day. Two or three, if they could also get the colonel and the major.

They would not be carrying bombs but inert air-to-air missiles, making the aircraft considerably lighter than normal. This meant their Eagle E was virtually configured for air combat, despite the fact that they would be making a low-level run to dodge the fully functioning radars dotted out there on the desert weapons range. The object of the exercise was not to be caught by them, or to so jam their opponents' sensors that in a hot situation in a real theatre of war the surface-to-air-missiles would not get off the ground, or miss altogether if they did.

The people waiting in the desert for them to make mistakes loved catching out hot-shot Eagle crews, as Garner knew only too well. He also knew Robert E. would be assessing their performance, even as the wily colonel prepared to catch them napping, and he was determined they would not be caught out.

As for the inert air-to-air missiles they carried, these dummy weapons would perform as if in real combat, without actually firing; but they would record the results as if they had been. If the Echo Eagle killed, it would be there for all to see. No Adversary jock would be able to argue his way out of the evidence.

Trussed up in their olive-green flight gear, they walked out towards their Eagle. As he strode next to Adderly, Garner suddenly remembered an instructor from the early days of conversion training on the F-15E. The instructor had put on display a life-sized illustration of the full kit necessary for flying an Eagle.

'What the well-dressed pilot or wizzo should wear,' he'd begun drily, then gone on to point out the various items that went to make up the entire outfit. 'Without this piece of tailoring you're a dead duck up there. *Always* check to make sure you've got it right. Check for the full integrity of your survival gear. Punching out is not the time to discover something is missing, or not working properly.

'Note this, people . . . nobody's going to give you a replacement while you're up in the wide blue; and though I know Ego drivers and back-seaters think they've got a direct line to the big Chief upstairs, *He* has not yet given you the ability to walk on air. You cannot leap buildings with a single bound. Thou art not God. Soft mortals like us need assistance to survive in His environment. A lot of very smart people have constructed your fashionable outfits. *Take care of them. Check them, and check again.* When I was somewhere near the age of you eager tenderfeet, I made a mistake. I was lucky to survive. You may not be.'

Garner had taken the warning to heart. Unconsciously, he ran a hand over his suit, checking for anomalies.

Arlene, with her well-honed intuition, had been right about the similarity between them. Both were roughly the same height at two inches under six feet. Both had slim, muscled frames with strong shoulders. Both had grey eyes and both, if one looked closely enough, had remarkably similar features. They even walked with a recognizable and indeed similar gait. But neither would accept it, if this was pointed out.

Their crew chief was waiting, in khaki T-shirt, camouflaged trousers and soft-soled boots. He would have already done his customary fine-toothcomb, pre-flight inspection; but it was still up to the aircrew to satisfy themselves with their own inspection. Standing next to the crew chief was a member of the ground crew, similarly dressed, attached to the aircraft by the umbilical cord of his headphones and mike. Through this, the ground crewman would talk to the aircrew while they went through their internal checks. But to begin with, the vital externals had to be done.

Garner glanced up at the stencil of their names, beneath the left rim of the one-piece curved windscreen. The cartoon profile of the head of an eagle was attached to an oblong box of a body. Within the box was the legend:

CAPT NATHAN ADDERLY
CAPT MILTON GARNER

Adderly began the walk-round of the aircraft while Garner climbed up to get on to the wing to ensure no items of maintenance equipment had been left there. It was not unknown with other aircraft – despite the inspections – for a forgotten spanner to slide its way between the slots of a flap or aileron, a possible guarantee of a hasty exit at altitude, or perilously close to the ground, later on.

This had never happened to Garner and Adderly, and they had no intention of letting it. Garner checked the wing surface for distortions, missing panels and so on. He checked that the huge blade of the dorsal air brake fitted its slot properly, and that there were no distortions that might affect its smooth deployment. Every minute detail had to be checked out for the safe operation of the aircraft.

On the ground, Adderly's inspection had taken him to the tail. He looked up at the huge engine nozzles looming above him. Grabbing a rim, he jumped briefly upwards to peer inside for loose articles. People tended to forget things in there too. He repeated the action with the second engine, looking for all the world as if doing a pre-flight workout.

Each cavernous circle of the Pratt and Whitney F-100 turbofans, as wide as half a man, could, on full afterburning thrust, hurl the massive aircraft vertically towards the heavens at 50,000 feet per minute: 570 miles an hour straight up. The Eagle E could do standing on its tail what the average airliner struggled to reach in level flight; faster than a cruising 747. If need be, it could hit Mach 2.5, yet it could also dawdle at 200 knots.

'All that,' Garner was fond of saying, 'and as agile as hell. Flyer heaven.'

They eventually completed their inspections and, satisfied, signed the 781 on the crew chief's clipboard. They were now accepting the aircraft. From now on until they brought it back in one piece and handed it over, it was their responsibility.

Garner climbed into the rear cockpit and settled into the zero-zero ejection seat. If for any reason he needed to eject, as with the front seat he could make his exit at high altitude, or at ground level. High-altitude ejection was not a choice he ever wanted to face.

In the front seat, Adderly began to swiftly do his cockpit checks. It was quite a cockpit. Roomy and bristling with the latest high-tech equipment, it was a fighter pilot's dream. The advanced head-up display, mounted at eye-level, was the widest HUD he'd ever seen. Its many modes would display all the essential information he would need at any given time, to enable him to fly the aircraft to the limits of his and its ability.

Below the head-up display were four flat panel displays. These were multi-function units and were virtually the instrument panel itself; a far cry from the relatively cluttered cockpit of the standard F-15. The two main displays, each with several menus, flanked the central control panel with its alphanumeric keypad sited directly beneath its vertically arranged, six-line data read-out strips. This was the up-front control panel through which virtually everything was programmed. It was the brains of the aircraft.

There was another item that was not so welcome for the crew: a voice. It was a female voice – chosen, it seemed, to be deliberately annoying – that warned them when things were getting too close for comfort. They called it Bitching Betty, and could do nothing about it.

Beneath the 'up-front' was another display, full colour and smaller than the main ones. This was currently showing the horizontal display map with the aircraft's position marked at the beginning of the programmed waypoint diagram. As the aircraft moved, so would its position on the map change in response.

An instrument's width over to the right of that display was the smallest of all. This contained the digital read-outs for the engines, among which were rpm, temperature and nozzle positions.

Adderly's left and right hands fell easily upon the throttles and stick. Covered in a plethora of buttons and switches, they would enable him to operate all the essential controls during hard-manoeuvring combat, without once having to remove them from there, even to change a page on one of the displays or arm a weapon. Convenient when your hands would at times weigh several times the norm, usually in a situation where you'd need to move them swiftly.

He rapidly checked the few analogue stand-by instruments that still remained from the older versions of the aeroplane, then prepared for engine start.

In the back seat, Garner also had four displays to occupy him. These were arranged horizontally: the two main ones in the centre, flanked by a slightly smaller display on either side. All the multi-page menus were interchangeable, between displays, and between cockpits.

Across the top of his cockpit, just forward of the instrument glare shield, was a solid grab bar that roughly followed the contours of the instrument panel, a shallow U-shape mounted upside down. The rear cockpit also had an up-front control, but this was positioned over on the forward section of the right console.

Immediately to the right of that was the black and yellow, T-shaped handle for the eject-mode seat control. It had three positions: normal was vertical. This enabled both seats to leave the aircraft, whoever pulled the handle. Forty-five degrees left position, was solo. This would mean that only the person wanting to leave the aircraft would go. Bad news for whoever was left behind.

The third position – aft initiate – ninety degrees to the left, gave the back-seater the command. In a situation where the pilot was incapacitated, or the aircraft was too low for him to let go of the controls and grab at the seat handles, the wizzo could still get him out.

Garner, in addition to his two hand controllers for the operation of his displays, also had a full set of controls to enable him to fly the aircraft, again in case of pilot incapacitation. He called them his security blanket.

3

Harnesses secured, helmets comfortable, masks on, gloves on, visors down.

Adderly reached to his right on the console by the edge of the seat, and moved the right engine generator switch to the ON position. He then reached forward for the T-shaped handle of the jet fuel starter lever on the bottom right of the instrument panel, and pulled. Almost simultaneously, his left hand moved the right throttle lever forward past the IDLE detent. He watched the engine display screen as the engine spooled up to fifty per cent rpm. The JFS disengaged and recharged. He repeated the procedure for the left engine. The Eagle woke up and was alive.

In the back seat, Garner initiated the built-in test sequence and began to set up his screens. The aircraft went through its BITE checks and on one of the main displays the read-outs began to show the status of the various systems by listing them as the Echo Eagle checked itself out.

Garner watched all this on his multi-function displays, which the air force liked to call CRTs – cathode ray tubes – and got all his systems on-line. He had his own less-than-respectful interpretation of the term; so he called the CRTs 'crits' and sometimes 'critters', as the mood took him. He now checked them out thoroughly, ensuring the inertial navigation system knew where it was starting from, meticulously working through all the aids that enabled him to operate the aircraft, in conjunction with the man in the driving seat up front. Adderly's own CRTs would be carrying repeated displays.

Adderly continued with his own programme in the front office, checking the flying controls for full and free movement, opening and closing the huge air brake to ensure its smooth operation. They checked the flying controls of both cockpits. Very bad news indeed if something were to happen to Adderly and Garner found he could not control the aircraft because they'd omitted to ensure everything worked while still safely on the ground.

The ground crewman unplugged himself from the aircraft and came to attention to give a smart salute. Adderly responded. They were ready to roll.

He began taxiing, lowering the big clamshell canopy as he did so. The noise of the engines was immediately muted, but their smoothly powerful vibrations coursed through the airframe.

Adderly looked left and right, ensuring the Eagle was clear of obstructions as they rolled forwards. In the back, Garner followed suit, double-checking their freedom of passage. They stopped a short distance later as attendant ground crew made final visual checks. No leaks, no loose missiles. People had been known to take off with loose ordnance, only to have them drop off in very embarrassing – and sometimes dangerous – circumstances.

But in their case everything was OK. Now they really were clear. They taxied out to the runway threshold. In the Arizona heat a haze seemed to rise from the surface of the vast 'road' as it stretched into the distance.

Then Adderly shoved the throttles into 'burner.

The Echo Eagle began to surge forwards, accelerating rapidly as twin tongues of flame seared into the baking air thirty feet behind them. The big E roared down the wide concrete.

Because of the relative lightness of armament load, the main wheels left the runway at 165 knots – instead of closer to 185 with a full warload – and Adderly reached ahead of the throttles for the small, red-wheeled lever to raise the gear swiftly, as speed increased relentlessly. He watched as the numerals in the oblong airspeed box on the HUD whirled themselves upwards dementedly.

'Gear up and locked,' he heard Garner confirm on the headphones.

'Roger. Gear locked.'

Adderly gave a firm pull on the stick then centred it, holding the attitude.

Momentarily punishing them with a sudden slam of increased G, the Eagle pointed its nose to the clear, bright sky, stood on its tail and headed for the upper reaches.

Garner always enjoyed these take-offs. As he stared past the back of Adderly's ejection seat to the deep blue of the sky, seemingly impaled on the nose of the aircraft, Garner reflected upon how accomplished a pilot the man in that seat really was. When it came to driving the Echo Eagle, Adderly was very hard to beat. If there was any pilot likely to ruin both Robert E.'s and 'Killer' Carter's day, it would be Adderly.

*   *   *

Fifty miles south of the base, they were approaching the northern boundary of the weapons range.

'Waypoint two in one minute,' Garner said. 'On your screen.'

'Roger,' Adderly acknowledged as the entire waypoint diagram appeared on one of his displays, superimposed on the moving map. On another CRT, the green waypoint diagram appeared by itself then expanded until only the current waypoint showed, with time to destination counting down at the top of the screen. 'Confirm.'

He knew that Garner's manipulation of the systems was exceptional and left all the navigation, planning and pre-merge battle tactics to him in the air-to-air role; and in the attack role, all the way to target. Garner had never let him down. He just wished there was a way to resolve the slavery business between them.

Adderly felt no guilt about the fact that he was descended from a slave-owning family. He was proud of his ancestor Josiah, who'd taken a radical step without even realizing it. Josiah had responded to his conscience and had simply brought to an inevitable conclusion the events that had put their mark upon him from boyhood. On a fateful day ten years before the

Civil War, he had been forced by his father to watch the gutting of the young slave who had been accused of raping his sister. Tears streaming down his cheeks, he had been a mere twelve years old at the time.

Always wanting a son but cursed – as Nathan Adderly had seen it – by a succession of daughters, Josiah had arrived late on the scene to a father who had grown too old to be a sympathetic parent during his son's childhood years. A true nineteenth-century patriarch with all the rigid attitudes of the time, he would not have tolerated any views other than his own. It was thus doubtful whether he would ever have been an understanding father.

Josiah's grooming to become a slave owner had thus begun very early. The pressure-cooker treatment had only succeeded in filling the boy with revulsion for the practice, turning him for ever against slavery; but he'd been smart enough to keep it well hidden from his brutal father. He'd done other things, too, that his father never suspected.

Josiah had never forgotten the experience of that appalling execution. When his father had been killed years later, by vengeful slaves whose suffering had driven them beyond despair and care for their own fate, he'd responded, on inheriting the plantation, by freeing them all. It had been just a year before the Civil War brought devastation upon the South. None of the former slaves had gone away, but had instead remained to continue working for him as free people. But the inexorable nature of war had destroyed the plantation, and the Adderlys had lost all the wealth that had taken generations to build. Josiah had looked upon the outcome as a kind of justice, before the Civil War had claimed him too. He'd succumbed to a wound, years after it had ended.

Adderly banked hard on to the new heading, as the next waypoint appeared on screen. It would soon be time to descend towards the barren Arizona peaks, thousands of feet below.

'I've been thinking,' came Garner's voice in his ear.

'I'm listening.'

'I don't think ol' Robert E.'s going to let us make the low run first. I think that sucker's going to bounce us *before* we descend. He's going to reckon we'll be too occupied, and won't be expecting it.'

'I agree. So what do we do?'

'We look below. He's down there somewhere. I can feel it.'

Adderly did not argue. He trusted Garner's instincts completely.

'Let's have a look,' he said.

It was Garner who made the first sighting.

'Got him!' he called. 'Low, low down. Five o'clock.'

He had seen the barest flitting of something down among the peaks off his right shoulder, in their five o'clock position. Whoever it was clearly intended to manoeuvre behind them, hoping to slide unnoticed into the six o'clock position behind the tail, before racing upwards for a sneaky kill. Dempsey had decreed that the air-to-air exercise would be simulated guns only, in the first engagement. This meant they did not have the benefit of an arm's-length kill with a missile shot. It was thus going to be a knife fight.

The tricky colonel obviously intended to make it as hard as possible for them. A knife fight in the big Eagle versus the much smaller, agile F-16 would be stacking the odds against them. A knife fight forced you to go slow, and slower still. In the Eagle, it was much better to be able to use all that power, to maximize the assets, and to take the opponent in very quick order.

Turning and burning wasted time and fuel, and tied you up for the bogey's friend to stand back and zap you while you were thinking you had his pal snarled up. Laughing all the way to a hole in the ground in real combat, in admiration of your fantastic flying, was not an option if his friend had got you in the meantime.

Dempsey, Garner knew, was well aware of that and wanted to drag them into a box where the F-16's considerable talents would begin to gain the upper hand, and perhaps set them up for a shot by the sadistic Major 'Killer' Carter. One of Carter's favourite sayings was 'gun their brains out'. Many a hot-shot, single-seat F-15 jock had been routinely taken by the old Aggressor F-5 pilots. The F-5 was a small, and basically simple, advanced trainer that had made it to fighter status in many air forces of smaller countries. The fact that the very able pilots who flew them could trounce more advanced machines was graphic proof of their deadliness.

Garner was thus very well aware of the even more deadly nature of the F-16s being flown by two of the hottest of the hot pilots around, as was Adderly. Garner also felt certain that the aircraft shadowing them at low level was piloted by Dempsey.

The colonel hadn't said they couldn't use their radar. However, in a hostile environment too much use of the radar would leave a calling card no self-respecting surface-to-air missile crew could afford to ignore. It was another lesson the colonel was forcing upon them, making them use their instincts instead of relying too much on all the technical wizardry at their fingertips. The technical aids were just that.

'Technology is your handmaiden,' Dempsey had pounded into their heads. 'Not your boss. Use them to *augment* your God-given instincts, and the training you have received. Become too dependent and if you should suffer even light battle damage, you become useless, and we lose a $44-million airplane; and possibly, two expensive crewmen. Airplanes we can build. Aircrews . . .' There had never been any need for him to continue.

So it would have to be mainly eyeball stuff in the coming fight, Garner reasoned.

'Happy to oblige,' he now murmured.

He briefly checked the radars to see if anything else was stooging around out there; but nothing showed. He put the radars on stand-by, leaving them ready for use, but not transmitting.

'OK,' Adderly was saying. 'I've got the systems. Let me know what he does.'

'You got it.'

Now that close-in combat was about to be joined, Adderly had command of the aircraft systems for that regime. Everything would now depend on his skills and instincts as a fighter pilot. Garner, meanwhile, would also be keeping his eyes out of the cockpit, sharing the lookout with Adderly, watching out for the Adversary, making sure that Adderly had full awareness of what the threat was doing. Four eyes were always better than two.

'Whoever is down there,' Adderly said, 'is going to have a buddy up top.'

Garner had already come to that conclusion and was surveying the air above them.

'Looking,' he said, 'but so far, diddly squat. But someone's up there all right.'

'OK. How's the low boy doing?'

Garner looked. 'He's still playing possum. Reckon he thinks we haven't seen him. My scalp says it's the colonel.'

'Your scalp may be right.'

Adderly had not yet given any overt indication that the sneaky F-16 had been spotted. He wanted to be sure of where the second, or perhaps even a third, might be.

Garner did another swift check of the sky above. He grabbed at the sturdy bar above the instrument panel for support, leaned forward to allow the inertia reel system to extend his harness, then twisted slightly round to check above and behind the tail. The exceptional vision afforded by the big canopy and the vast space between the fins enabled him to have a perfect view of the danger area.

Something flashed minutely, high up, then was gone.

'Oh yeah!' he said, still twisted round.

'Something?'

'Oh yes, indeed. *Some*thing. Company. Six o'clock and pretty high. Bet he thinks he's smart.'

'What's he doing?'

'Nothing yet, but I think he's going to be the decoy. He'll try a bounce and when he believes we're spooked and focused on him, the guy below will come up for a bite of our ass.'

'Or the other way round.'

'Yeah.' Garner agreed. He had turned round again, and had settled back in his seat.

'OK,' Adderly repeated. 'Let's see how smart they are.'

Adderly lit the 'burners suddenly and hauled the Eagle into a steep climb. The aircraft's phenomenal power had it standing on its tail once more. But Adderly kept a firm back pressure on the stick and the F-15E began to bring its nose past the vertical, until it was climbing at a steep angle in a reverse direction, upside down. He eased the pressure then rolled upright. They were now hurtling towards where Garner had seen the flash.

Garner's four CRTs had twenty push buttons each, arranged around each screen, in groups of five. Additionally, there were three rocker switches – again on the borders of each display – controlling on-off, brightness and contrast. But much of the work was done via the two fixed controllers – one on each side console – which looked like joysticks, housing their own plethora of buttons and switches. This made life easier and enabled Garner to work his screens, even under heavy manoeuvring conditions.

He could have gone for a brief flash of the radar for a quick scan, but had no wish to warn whoever was up there by setting off in response the Falcon's radar warning receiver. He decided to occupy himself by keeping his eyes out of the cockpit, hunting out their still-invisible adversary.

Something flashed in the distance once more, this time heading earthwards.

'He's made us,' Garner announced. 'He's

decided not to commit for now, and is heading for the deck.'

'Got him. What's his buddy doing?'

Garner had a quick look. A nimble shape was in a fast climb. 'Coming up.'

'Going for the sucker punch, are they? Well, not this kid. Going down!'

Adderly rolled the big fighter and pulled hard towards the primeval spines of the parched mountains far beneath them.

Garner continued to resist the desire to give a quick sweep of the powerful radar. The colonel wanted it the tough way. That was what the colonel was going to get.

He looked at the olive-brown terrain expanding towards him; saw the large tract of a dried river-bed with the familiar etchings of paths that crossed each other in wild patterns, reminding him of a child's first attempts at drawing. Almost like his own, he thought detachedly. He saw a paved road curving gently through the mountains. Here and there, tiny clusters of buildings branched haphazardly off it.

Then the Eagle was being wrenched to the right and the world pivoted as Adderly turned hard on to the tail of the ascending Falcon. But the move had been spotted early and the Falcon was twinkling away to the left, seemingly to fall out of the sky as it flashed out of the targeting box on the Eagle's HUD.

'Where ... where's his buddy?' Adderly grunted as he went into a body-punishing turn to follow.

Garner saw 7.5G registered on the meter for the briefest of instants. Even without that information, the sudden, giant-hand pressure on his body would have told him.

The G-forces went back to normal, but that would not last for long. When Adderly's air-fighting blood was up, being in a state of 1G for any appreciable length of time was a luxury.

'Down among the rocks,' Garner replied. 'Three o'clock. Through that valley, there.'

A shape, camouflaged to blend with the desert scenery, was fleeing along a narrow cleft. The other F-16 seemed to have disappeared ...

'*Break hard left!*' Garner shouted.

Adderly did not question the call and reacted instantly. The world tumbled. Earth changed places with sky, then back again. The big Eagle was in a steep climb on the 'burners, then it was hauling itself off the top of a loop. As the nose began to come down once more, Adderly rolled ninety degrees and pulled tightly into another left turn.

The Falcon he had broken away from flashed by at a shallow angle just off the nose, going the other way.

'Holy shit!' Garner exclaimed as the shape hurtled past. 'That was close! Speed of light!'

'You wish. That was a good call.'

'Aim to please. He nearly suckered us though. He was real sneaky.'

'"Nearly" is a miss. Good enough for me. Now let's put this joker out of his misery. Keep an eye on the guy down there in the dirt.'

'I got him . . . and he's on his way up. I guess they're talking to each other, trying to corral us. We'd better get his buddy quick before he gets here.'

'I'm on him.'

Adderly had hit the air brake as he'd banked into another punishing turn to follow the Falcon. The huge panel on the spine had deployed, slowing the Eagle as if it had slammed against a brick wall, and allowing Adderly to reef the aircraft round on a wingtip. Then the air brake was going back in and the 'burners came on. The Eagle leapt after its prey.

The Falcon, meanwhile, was already into its own turn, aiming to get back on the Eagle's tail. But Adderly had gone high and the Echo Eagle was now upside down and both he and

Garner were looking through the top of the canopy, down at the Falcon, which was by now wrenching round into its turn, looking for the fat Eagle.

Adderly eased the stick gently backwards. The Eagle's nose began to inch down, following the Falcon precisely. The symbology on the HUD began to indicate that he was getting close to a gun solution.

Don't rush it, he said in his mind. Easy. Easy.

It wouldn't do to miss the shot now, after having sweated to get into a nice position for the kill.

To someone standing outside with a God's-eye view, the entire manoeuvre was unfolding with astonishing rapidity. But in the cockpit it was as if the Eagle and the Falcon were standing still as in a split second Adderly matched momentum with the aircraft beneath him.

The tone sounded just as he squeezed the trigger. A perfect kill. In a real shoot, the Falcon would have been straddled from nose to tail. The Falcon pilot made no comment over the air, but both felt certain his cockpit was probably blue with expletives.

'*Yes!*' Garner exulted. '*We got him!*'

Adderly did not waste time gloating but had

already broken off the attack, to hunt out the second Falcon.

'Where's his buddy now?' he asked tersely.

Garner had again swivelled round. 'Trying to waltz into our six. He's not there yet. Seven o'clock, coming down.'

Adderly glanced over his left shoulder even as he was again reefing the Eagle into a hard left-hander, and spotted the F-16 curving down. Its chance spoiled, the Falcon rolled out of the turn and disappeared to their right, still going down.

Adderly fell after him and began to gain. But the Falcon had leapt into a rocket-like climb and shot past their nose, going straight up. Adderly kept going down.

'*What are you doing?*' Garner was once more looking at the ground rushing up. 'He's going to come over the top and follow us down!'

'Yep.'

'*Yep?* What if it's old Robert E. himself?'

'We've either just got him, or the crazy major. Either way, our chances have improved.'

'You reckon whoever's in that bird knows that? And does he care? He's out for a piece of our butt.'

'And I'm after his head. What's he doing now?'

Garner glanced back and up at the receding sky. 'We've got a tail, and it's Falcon-shaped. Gawd! That bird looks mean as hell from this angle.'

Adderly rolled a full 180 degrees in the dive and began to pull. The Eagle continued to drop, but the nose was beginning to curve through, though with some reluctance as the phenomenal momentum continued to drag them earthwards. Soon they were plunging vertically; then the nose was creeping past the vertical. Yet ground still seemed to be rushing straight at them, still on the nose.

Those damn mountain peaks are beginning to look very, very hungry, Garner thought calmly.

He stared at the brown earth, and said nothing. He forced his head round. The Falcon was still hanging on, but was not close enough for guns.

The ground was beginning to look close enough to touch. A peak to the right was definitely too close. The Eagle's nose had now crept upwards, making the dive shallow. Adderly was still hauling on the stick. The G-forces were squeezing at them. The Eagle itself seem quite happy to hit them with as much as they could stand – and more.

They flashed past the mountain peak and hurtled, in level flight now, into its valley.

Garner let out his breath slowly and caught a sudden, great mouthful of oxygen as he instinctively inhaled, unaware he'd been holding his breath.

'What's he doing?' Adderly grunted.

Garner had taken another look behind the tail. The Falcon had pulled away just above the peak, over whose spine it was now skimming.

'He's bugged out! He's on that peak. Go get him!'

Adderly grinned, without humour, in his mask. He'd been hoping for that. He brought the throttles briefly back, hit the air brake and, as the big aircraft slowed, hauled the nose slightly up and curved towards the peak, closing the air brake as he did so, and increasing speed to slide neatly into the Falcon's six.

The tone came almost immediately.

The Falcon rolled frantically, but it was far too late.

'Goddamit!' they heard. It was 'Killer' Carter.

'Hell,' Adderly exclaimed softly in wonder. 'We got the colonel first. Wow!'

'Good stuff, Nathan. Good stuff.'

'You weren't so bad yourself.'

'Yeah.'

As if afraid of this sudden rush of bonhomie, they fell silent. In the air, however, despite the antipathy generated by their ancestral histories, there was a contract between them. Each knew that neither would let the other down, no matter what. This covered all aspects of their flying. To break that unwritten contract would be beyond the pale.

Then Garner began working the screens. 'I'm setting up the low-level run now,' he told Adderly briskly. 'We'll do RAF altitudes, instead of standard TF. That OK with you?'

'It's OK with me.'

Though the normal Echo Eagle low-level attack altitude under terrain-following control was 350 feet, Garner and Adderly tended to emulate the RAF Tornado crews and go as low as they dared. If they were not doing a stand-off attack, fifty feet was their usual above-ground-level height, which Adderly flew manually. This gave them an added bonus. No TF at ultra-low AGL meant no returns to alert the bad boys. It allowed them to sneak up on the target and do the dirty, before being picked up on radar; by which time they'd be well away out of the hot area. Today they were going to do the ultra-low run. The intention was to beat the training SAMs and the eager anti-aircraft crews, waiting for them out there in the desert and among the mountains.

'Waypoints on your screen,' Garner said.

Adderly saw the new waypoint pattern appear, with symbols where each SAM and anti-aircraft artillery was expected to be. Their route in and out should take them safely past all the known threat areas.

That still left mobile and hand-held missiles, as well as mobile triple-A. They'd just have to be quick with the electronic countermeasures and jam any searching radars that tried to snare them. The trouble with flooding the frequencies with ECM was that in a real situation, even if the enemy couldn't locate you he'd still know you were out there somewhere.

This was not to be an attack run. The colonel had been quite specific. The task they were training for was not an attack mission. The prime requirement was *avoidance*. The radar and SAMs were not supposed to know they were there; or at the very least, be unable to get a lock on them while they flashed through.

'Let's do it,' Adderly said, and took the Eagle low.

'So far so good,' Garner said moments later.

Adderly banked the Eagle to thread their way between two claw-faced, reddish-brown perpendicular walls and wondered whether the storm of their passage would start a rock slide. Then they were through and coming out over wide, open ground.

'Hope it stays that way,' Adderly said.

They were heading for waypoint four on the plan that Garner had programmed, and had managed to avoid being detected. Four more to go and they'd be home and dry. But the wide, flat valley they were now hurtling over was a risk. He'd inserted that particular waypoint because, according to the information supplied at the briefing, this section of the range was clear of anti-aircraft weaponry. That did not mean it was *absolutely* clear. Simulated threat or not, the unexpected was always to be expected.

As with all things to do with combat, intelligence received could be out of date less than a minute after receipt. The cunning people manning the training radars were justly famous for their nasty little tricks. They could easily have positioned a mobile SAM out there, somewhere, just for the hell of it; just nicely positioned to catch out overconfident, hot-shot Echo Eagle crews.

Garner did not want to call a pop-up, so that

he could flash the Eagle's exceedingly powerful APG-70 radar to make a quick grab at anything that might have sneaked into the area. Doing that would inevitably send the lurking SAM crews' own warning systems berserk, and these would in turn swiftly start hunting for the interloper. One more fish in the net.

'Not us,' Garner muttered.

'Say what?'

'Just wondering if there's a sneaky SAM out there,' he replied.

The waypoints he'd set up had nicely avoided all attention – so far. They had slid between mountains, roared along dried river-beds, squeezed between rock faces, putting solid ground between them and the hopeful radars – until now.

'We'll soon find out if there is,' Adderly said.

'Yeah.'

Garner had gambled on the route, knowing that at the mouth of at least one canyon, someone would have had the bright idea to position a SAM site. He'd pored over the topo map of the area and had made his choices. For waypoints four to five he'd decided to risk open ground. They'd never expect something so crazy. He hoped.

Adderly was considering the same odds. 'Hope you guessed right,' he said.

'Yeah,' he repeated.

To anyone watching, they appeared to be skating along the desert floor at suicidal speed, so low had Adderly taken the aircraft. If a radar was indeed hiding out there, it would find it very difficult to acquire the Eagle E.

Because of the extremely low altitude, Bitching Betty was going crazy in their ears, warning them of their perilous proximity to the ground. She castigated them every time she thought her precious Eagle was being put at risk by its crazy crew, and she *always* sounded pissed off.

They ignored her.

The Eagle's big wing made the ride a little rough as it raced through the heavy air. This low down, it could never compete for ride quality with the likes of the variable sweep F-111, or the Tornado. But both Garner and Adderly had long ago accepted that. Better a rough ride low down coupled with astounding power and agility at virtually all altitudes, than the reverse, with – relatively speaking – the turning capability of a truck in mud.

Five miles ahead of them was a slot in the high terrain, within which they could hide once more. From waypoints five to six the run was through a deep valley that ran straight from point to point.

Garner willed the aircraft on. Despite their high speed, he felt exposed. The short distance to the safety of the mountain range seemed inordinately long.

But the radar warners stayed resolutely quiet. There were no lurking SAM radars trying to hook them. The naked ground was clear.

At last, they reached waypoint five and plunged into the hidden recess of the deep canyon.

Garner felt relief. It should be a milk run to home base from now on.

Then the radar warners gave a frantic beeping.

Goddamit! he thought.

The worst had happened. Someone had been smart enough to plant a SAM site right at the exit.

Damn! Damn! Damn!

Even as these thoughts hit him, he was shouting, '*Go up the left wall and over the top! Now, now, now! I'm hitting ECM!*'

Adderly did not waste valuable energy in acknowledgement.

As Garner began jamming the offending

radar, he reacted instantly and hauled the Eagle steeply up, rolled over the top of the canyon and dropped breathtakingly down the other, equally steep wall, to curve into another deep gorge. Then he rolled the aircraft upright.

The beeping had stopped.

Garner's heart was pounding. 'You big beautiful bird!' he said to the Eagle exultantly, patting the instrument panel as he would a favourite horse, or even his Boss Mustang. 'I'm modifying the other waypoints,' he went on to Adderly. 'Sheee-it! That was close. They didn't get a lock-on. Good stuff. Good stuff there, driver.'

'Sharp call,' Adderly responded. 'That was pretty hot too.'

'Yeah. Not bad, if I say so myself. New waypoint pattern coming up. On your screen.'

'Got it. Was that some nasty little surprise. Reckon they've got more rigged up for us?'

'Could be. Could be.'

But Garner's new waypoints did the trick. The remainder of the run was clear, all the way back to base.

4

The colonel and the major were waiting for them in debriefing. They were the only Eagle crew in the room. The major was in flight overalls, but Dempsey was in uniform.

Dempsey looked thoughtfully at them, stroking the tip of his nose with a forefinger. He stopped, and placed both hands on his hips.

'Gentlemen,' the deep voice began. 'You did good up there. Very impressive.' He glanced at Carter. 'You got Major Carter, and the other bogey.'

Carter did not look pleased.

Dempsey stared at them. 'You seem surprised, *and* disappointed, gentlemen. Am I to believe you hoped for a kill on me? Did you think I was up there too?'

'Well, sir . . .' Adderly began. 'You did say . . .'

'I don't remember specifying which aircraft I'd be flying.'

'Yes, sir . . . I mean, no, sir.'

'Exactly. As I was saying, you did good but . . .' The eyes stared hard at them. 'My little surprise with the SAM caught you out. I contacted the range personnel and set it up once you were airborne, just in case. You entered the trap. In a real situation you would have been caught in that canyon and even if you had managed to evade as successfully as you did out there today, every fighter airfield within a hundred miles would have sent the hunters out. In short, gentlemen, you would have been compromised, and in deep doo-doo.'

'Sir,' Garner and Adderly said together.

Then Dempsey relented. 'As it was the only mistake – which, I accept, you quickly rectified – all things considered, you had a good day, gentlemen. But don't go sitting on your laurels, or giving them a good polish. Get some rest and be ready for your next hop. Who knows? You might come up against me tonight. Thank you, gentlemen.'

'Sir,' they again said together, and went out.

When they'd left, Carter said, 'Why didn't you tell them they'd got you too?' He sounded aggrieved.

'Keeps them on their toes,' Dempsey replied

unrepentantly. 'They thought they'd scored a major victory. Knowing they got the colonel's head would have caused them to relax. I can't allow that. Your head's trophy enough for now.'

'Gee. Thanks!'

'Don't take it so hard, Major. You got hit by a pair of real stars. Nearly put you into that mountain, didn't they? These boys play hard. I like that. We've got our first team. The only other crew who come close are our Californian beach god, Lancer, and his wizzo, Hershon. Unless, of course, they foul up today. So for the moment, assuming things don't change, they're our stand-by if something goes wrong with the Jazz Couple.'

'Seems like your mind's already made up. So we're cancelling the night hop?'

'No, we're not. The programme continues until there's absolutely no doubt we've got what we're looking for. The night hop's the most important of all.'

'Nice man,' Garner said drily, as they walked away from the briefing room.

'Look at it this way . . . he didn't chew us out for getting tagged by that SAM radar. Still, I'd hoped we'd got him.'

'We got him,' Garner said quietly.

Adderly glanced at him, not quite certain whether to give any serious credence to the remark. 'What do you mean? He hasn't been up. He's in uniform.'

'Yeah. He's throwing us a curve. Didn't you see his feet?'

'Why should I look at his feet?'

'He was in uniform, but he was wearing flying boots.'

'Perhaps he's getting ready . . .'

'Aw, c'mon. The *colonel*? Mr Every-button-in-the-right-place? Give me a break.'

Adderly paused. 'If you're right . . . Of all the low-down . . .'

'You got it,' Garner said with a tight smile as they continued walking.

'Well, I'll be . . . So we did get the head of Robert E. Hah! Wonder if he'd ever tell us.'

'I suggest we tell no one until this is over. *He* won't realize we already know. That gives us an edge. He's going to try something sneaky again tonight. I can feel it.'

'Well, then, let's see if we can get us a bird colonel twice in one day.'

'You're playing my tune.'

*　　*　　*

Garner spent much of the time before their next flight working on the Mustang. The air policeman, Mason Lyle, was very eager to help.

Adderly made a long call to his wife. After they'd been speaking for half an hour or so, she wanted to know when he'd be coming home.

'Can't say for sure, sweetheart,' he told her. 'You know how it is.'

'Sure I know, but I want you home, Nate.' She sounded petulant.

It was not like the old Arlene at all. He'd hoped that after the birth of the new baby she'd start getting back to her old self and stop feeling so guilty. But that didn't seem to be happening. Perhaps it was still too soon. She now watched the infant like a hawk, and was most reluctant to let anyone else hold him.

The only people she seemed happy to pass him to without hesitation were Adderly and, strangely, Garner.

But Garner did not come visiting so often any more.

As if she'd read what was going on in Adderly's mind, she said, 'You and Milt getting on OK?'

'We're OK. We did pretty well today. Tell you all about it when I get back.'

'It would be nice to see him come round again.'

'You'll have to take that up with him. He won't take an invite from me. You know that.'

'It's so foolish, Nate.'

'I guess he's got to work things out for himself.'

'I guess.'

There was the faint hum of electronics as they both fell silent for some moments.

'I love you, sweetheart,' he told her softly.

'I love you too, Nate.'

'Your mama with you?'

'She's here.'

'Need anything?'

'I need you with me.'

'I know.'

'Call me tonight?'

'I might be late . . .'

'I don't mind. Call as late as you want. You know I'll be here.'

'OK, sweetheart. I call tonight. Love you.'

'Love you, Nate.'

He waited for her to hang up, then hung up with a sigh.

*   *   *

Night time with the Echo Eagle was a whole new ball game. That was when the other aspects of its wondrous equipment came into their own. The Eagle had many eyes in the night and Garner loved trying to get the maximum out of the various modes of the aircraft's optical, radar and infrared systems.

The LANTIRN targeting and navigation pods gave him the ability to get to and see his targets on the blackest of nights. Up front, Adderly would be looking at the world through the FLIR's infrared window, superimposed on the HUD.

Low-altitude navigation and targeting infrared for night. A mouthful. LANTIRN was a lot easier to say.

Garner smiled in his mask as he thought of the acronym-speak necessary in the fighter jock world. FLIR. Forward-looking infrared. TACAN. Tactical air navigation. HSD. Horizontal situation display . . .

'You having fun back there?' came Adderly's voice.

'What?'

'Sounds like you're doing some kind of recitation.'

He hadn't realized he'd voiced his thoughts. 'Er . . . no. Just muttering while I move one of the waypoints.'

They were flying a little higher on this hop. Two hundred feet. On the far-left screen, he had put on the repeated HUD display, complete with infrared image. He could see the patch of the outside world that Adderly was looking at, as they hurtled through the Arizona night. They were not using the terrain-following radar, in order to minimize 'signature', and were again flying manually. Every so often, a warning would appear on the HUD, giving steering commands. At the moment, it was telling them to pull up.

Adderly eased the stick back slightly and the Eagle breasted a mean-looking outcrop whose infrared image was clearly seen.

'Wonder what Robert E. has planned for us this time,' Adderly said.

'Whatever it is, it won't be nice.'

'Amen to that.'

'At least we're allowed to go to missiles, so perhaps we'll zap him before he gets us. I think he'll come at us sometime during the run – maybe when we think we're home and dry he'll try to shut the door. He's sure mean enough to pull that one. Waypoint three. On screen.'

'Got it. All quiet,' Adderly went on, as the radar warning receiver stayed silent. 'So far, no tags. Looks like we've got another good pattern.'

'Yeah ... but we're not out of the woods yet.' Garner glanced up through the canopy. 'Nice bright starlight and ...' He paused.

'What? What?'

'*Climb! Climb!*' Garner shouted. 'And go 180. Select AMRAAM.'

''Burners in! Going up!' Adderly did not hesitate. Tongues of flame lit the night as the Echo Eagle roared skywards, streaking away from the rocks below. Then he pulled further on the stick. The aircraft began to curve into the beginnings of a loop. 'AMRAAM selected. So much for quiet! Every SAM will be on to us now. What did you see?'

The Eagle was now going in the opposite direction, on its back. Adderly rolled upright. He was ready for the simulated advanced medium-range missile shot, if things worked out.

Garner had switched on the air-to-air radar. 'Take a look at your screen.'

Adderly looked. 'Where did *he* come from?'

Using his sidestick controllers, Garner had moved the cursor to frame the target aircraft neatly, designating it; then he pressed the radar auto-acquisition switch. Almost immediately, the radar locked up the target.

'And we've got lock.'

On the HUD repeater, the target designator box appeared at top right.

Adderly had already begun to manoeuvre to bring the box within the missile's wide steering circle. Once in there, he'd get the shoot cue.

'How did you know he'd be there?' Adderly enquired.

'My scalp itched.'

'You didn't see him?'

'No. Watch him! He's heard the tone and is trying to break out.'

'I've got him. He's not getting away.'

Whoever was out there in the night was manoeuvring frantically, and jamming for all he was worth. Twice, the targeting box disappeared, only to appear once more at a different location on the HUD. Adderly was as good as his word. He had no intention of losing the target aircraft.

Then the radar warning went.

'Shit!' he muttered. 'A SAM's painting us! Break him!'

'You hang on to that guy,' Garner said as he began to jam the SAM radar. 'I've got those dead-beats down there trying to read the snow on their screens.'

'I'm hanging on! He's dancing all over the place.'

'Don't you lose him!'

Then another sound came. Ominous. A SAM had been 'fired'. Bitching Betty was also telling them all about it.

'Launch!' Garner called.

'I hear! Damn it!' Adderly continued, venting his frustration. Then their missile at last achieved full shooting parameters.

Adderly fired.

There was no need to keep radar lock now. The simulated missile would do its own thing and chase the target independently, as if it had been really fired. The computers – both on the aircraft and on the range – would have calculated the firing parameters, come to a precise conclusion about the result and relayed the information to the core of the simulation system back at the base, in real time.

'We're out of here!' Adderly said, flung the Eagle on to its back and headed earthwards. 'How's that SAM doing?' he grunted.

'You can hear it. It's still coming. Find us a nice mountain while I spoil its dinner.'

'You got it.'

As Adderly sent the Eagle rushing towards a peak he could see clearly on the infrared HUD display, Garner worked at jamming the missile. Then they were rushing through the darkness of a canyon and the missile warner abruptly went quiet. Bitching Betty sulked off.

Adderly sighed with relief. 'Well, we lost it, and maybe got whoever was out there too.'

'And we're compromised, as Robert E. would say.'

'Yeah. Damn it!'

'Back to the waypoint pattern,' Garner said. 'Let's see if we can get home without alerting any more SAMs, *or* the fighters.'

They made it back without further excitement, to discover they had indeed got the colonel a second time. But it was a pyrrhic victory.

'Good shooting, gentlemen,' he told them drily in the debriefing room. He stroked his nose briefly. 'Shame you got the SAMs all excited. What's wrong with that picture?'

Carter was standing to one side. Both senior officers were in their flying overalls.

'We're compromised?' Garner suggested tentatively.

'Indeed, Mr Garner. You are.'

Major Carter looked on with a smirk. He was also very pleased he was not the one who had taken their missile shot.

'Why did you turn to attack me?' Dempsey was asking. 'I had not swept you with my radar. For all you knew, I might have had no idea you were there, until you initiated the attack.'

'I called the attack, sir,' Garner said.

Dempsey fixed him with an unblinking stare. 'Why?'

Garner stood his ground. 'You were about to become a threat, sir.'

'But I gave no indication, Captain. I did not use my radar.'

'Only because we got to you first, sir.'

There was a sudden silence. Even Carter had stopped smirking, as they all waited for Dempsey's reaction.

Dempsey said nothing for some moments, his eyes never leaving Garner's. Then still without saying anything, he turned to a computer behind him which had a screen saver running, and tapped a key. Immediately, a generated image of the flight began to run on the large monitor.

'Download from the main debrief,' Dempsey explained. 'Watch carefully, gentlemen.'

All aspects of the flight were shown, with all the aircraft involved, and the terrain, displayed in wireframe. The Echo Eagle was outlined in blue, the pursuing Falcons in orange. The mountains, the desert floor, the SAM sites and radar units, all came up as the flight progressed. Each aircraft had wingtip trails, so that their manoeuvres could be graphically depicted.

One of the F-16s had clearly begun to stalk the Eagle and just as the latter pulled into its sudden climb, a coned pulse shot from the stalking F-16, missing the target altogether. Dempsey had used his radar an instant too late; but he'd used it.

The Eagle's completed manoeuvre then put it in a perfect position to get a fast lock on the by now desperately evading Falcon. The F-16's efforts were to no avail.

Then came the SAM lock, and the surface-to-air missile 'fired' at the Eagle. Soon after, the Eagle's own shot at the Falcon was displayed as a trail with the 'missile' at its head. It 'hit' the Falcon squarely, turning it into a little orange coffin. The colonel had bought it. This was then followed by the Eagle's own energetic avoidance manoeuvres as Adderly had lost height rapidly, to make for the safety of the canyon, towing the hungry SAM in its wake.

But Garner's jamming, plus Adderly's inspired manoeuvres, had worked and the 'missile' had impacted on high ground.

The replay ended.

Dempsey exited the programme and faced them once more.

'Good work,' he said, astonishing them. 'You used your instincts and caught me out. But you still alerted the SAMs. You'll have to think of a way to look after your butts, without exciting the SAMs. On the mission itself, *avoidance* is the key. Thank you, gentlemen. I'll give you my decision in the morning. Back here at 10.00 hours, on the button.'

They came to attention. 'Sir!' they said together, and to Carter, 'Major.'

Carter nodded at them.

As they began to leave, Dempsey said, 'By the way. I was up this afternoon. You got me.'

'We know,' Adderly said. 'You still had your flying boots on, sir.'

'I'll be damned,' Dempsey said to Carter as the two captains left. He smiled fleetingly, then slowly drew forefinger and thumb along his jawline. 'I'll be damned.'

Carter looked smug, and said nothing.

Adderly made his promised call to Arlene. She'd been eagerly waiting for it and they talked for a good hour. The baby was peacefully asleep. He knew that Arlene would be watching the child even as she spoke, alert to anything that might go wrong. He didn't think she was getting enough sleep herself.

He told her so.

'I'm OK,' she said. 'I don't need much.'

He wasn't convinced, but said nothing more about it. If the colonel picked him and Garner for the mission, he hoped he'd be able to spend a day or two with her before setting off.

But he wouldn't ask for special treatment. He didn't want anyone to think he was sloping off in order to attend to his family problems.

In the event, there was no need.

When they'd turned up at the briefing room, Dempsey surprised them by giving them three days off. Lancer and Hershon had also been called in.

'I want you all back on base, gentlemen,' Dempsey said to them, 'three days from now. Captain Adderly, Captain Garner, you get the first crack, and will be told the mission on your return. Are you happy with that?'

'Yes, sir!' they replied.

'Good. I want you both in here, at 10.00 hours, on day four. I do not expect you to be late. Mr Lancer, Mr Hershon,' Dempsey went on to the second crew, 'you will be on stand-by in case for any reason Garner and Adderly can't make it. You will be given details of the mission only when the situation arises. However, both ships will fly as a pair to the forward base. Mr Adderly.'

'Sir?'

'I've assumed you'd like to see your family, back at your home unit. There's an AFRes MAC flight heading in that direction in one hour. You've got a seat on it. Be there.'

A very surprised Adderly could not hide his pleasure. 'Yes, sir. Thank you, sir!'

'Just don't be late back.'

'That's a roger, sir,' Adderly vowed.

'I'll hold you to it. You've all done well,' Dempsey continued. 'As the requirement is for two crews, those who didn't get to this point are heading back to their units, knowing a little more about themselves. You were all good. It's been a privilege to work with you. And that's all, gentlemen. Enjoy your three days.'

Adderly caught the Air Force Reserve military airlift command flight Hercules C-130, to his base in North Carolina. Lancer and Hershon took a civilian flight north-west across the state border into Nevada, bound for Las Vegas for some serious entertainment. Garner decided to spend the free time working on the Mustang.

The air policeman, Lyle, would put in an

appearance from time to time, when he was off duty.

It was early evening when Adderly arrived home.

Arlene rushed to the door, wrapped her arms about him and hung on for several moments. He held her tightly. Her long and fine hair, bunched against his cheek, smelled fresh and intoxicating.

'I'm here, sweetheart,' he said gently. 'I'm here.' He held her face in his hands, kissed both her eyelids, then the full lips that had so captivated him when he'd first set eyes on her.

'Do you really have to go back so soon?' she asked, inclining her head back slightly, to look at him.

He nodded. 'Yes.'

She stiffened abruptly as the sound of Eagle Es taking off from the nearby base came to them. She relaxed again as the sounds faded.

She's still so jumpy, he thought.

'It's all right,' he soothed. He held her close, one arm about her waist as they moved further into the house.

She flashed him a quick smile. 'I'm OK. Really.'

'Come on. Show me the boy.'

'Mama's with him. He's asleep right now. He sleeps a lot.'

'That's good, isn't it?'

'I guess.'

They went up to their bedroom. Arlene had put the baby's cot right next to her side of the bed. Her mother, a very handsome woman who looked astonishingly like her, greeted Adderly with a warm smile.

'Nate,' she said, giving him a quick hug and a kiss on the cheek. 'Your boy's been good. He's fast asleep.' She even sounded like her daughter. 'Saving all that energy for when he grows up and becomes a fighter pilot, just like his daddy.'

'My son's not going to be a fighter pilot,' Arlene said sharply.

Adderly glanced urgently at his mother-in-law and signalled that she should make no comment. Nadine Labouchere nodded barely perceptibly, and left the bedroom.

'No one's going to make him do what he doesn't want to,' he said to Arlene as they approached the cot. He smiled proudly down at the infant boy. 'He's so beautiful,' he went on. 'Just like you. I can't believe it. Sometimes, I think I'm dreaming it all.'

'Are you happy with him, Nate? Really happy? There's nothing wrong with him, is there?' She frowned uncertainly at the baby. Her hand gripped his tightly, then relaxed.

'Happy? What do you think? I'm crazy about him. I'm crazy about you. And no, there's nothing wrong with him. He's perfect.' He continued to smile foolishly down at the baby, forcing himself not to pick up the child and so wake him. 'Hi there, John Milton,' he whispered. 'Daddy's home.'

Watching him touch a small hand very lightly, Arlene said, 'How's Milt?'

'He's OK.' Adderly stroked the baby's hand once more, then took his finger away. 'Working on that car of his.'

'It really exists?' She now seemed less anxious, as if talking about the car was a safer subject.

Adderly smiled at her. 'It really exists, and it really is a Boss Mustang. For a while there, I thought it was all part of his imagination and I was never going to see that thing for real. He's done a good job too, so far. He's even got himself an AP from the base – another Georgia man, and a certified Mustang nut – to help him. When I left, they were making like they were tuning it for a NASCAR race.'

'Have you told him yet, Nate?' She was

looking at him intently, her hand still loosely in his.

Adderly knew what she meant. He shook his head slowly.

'You should,' she insisted. 'He should know we named the baby after him.'

'I promise to tell him,' Adderly said after a pause. 'And I'll bring him here when we get back, whatever he says. This time, I won't take no for an answer. OK?'

She put her arms about him and leaned back, her pelvis pressed against him. It was something she used to do quite often before the first baby. It usually drove him wild, and was beginning to work.

'Good enough,' she said.

'And now,' he said, feeling a growing heat where their bodies met, 'can a man have a real welcome around here?'

'The baby,' she demurred half-heartedly. 'And there's Mama.'

'Somehow, I don't think your mama's going to come looking for us for a while. And as for young John here, he sleeps a lot, you said.'

Her smile came close to the way he remembered it used to be, when she was feeling sexy. 'I guess I did.'

He stroked her cheek. 'Are you going to be

OK with this?' His concern, despite his desire for her, was genuine.

After the death of the first baby, she'd once told him something was wrong with her down there. It had killed her little girl and therefore *she* was really responsible for what had happened. She hadn't said that since having the new baby but, even so, he'd always had the feeling she was primed to go off at any moment. He'd talked to the base MO about it.

'What she needs,' the doctor had said, 'is a lot of understanding, and plenty of loving. Deep within her mind, she believes you might be blaming her, just as she blames herself. She may get over it quickly, or it may take some time. Let her get through it. She'll sometimes think you don't find her attractive any more.

'You're going to have to show her you don't blame her, and that you do still find her very attractive. Just give her the love and reassurance she needs. From what I know of both your families, she has all the support she requires, and more. So just give her some time, and keep letting her know you're still crazy about her.'

Adderly had no problem with that. As he'd just said, he was crazy about her.

'What I mean . . .' he continued.

But she was kissing him, interrupting whatever he'd been about to say. 'Why don't you find out?'

He fell asleep that night a very happy man, with Arlene's moist and satisfied, naked body partially lying across his.

The baby slept all night.

'Mason,' Garner said on the second free day at the Arizona base.

The enlisted man was under the car, checking the hydraulics on a front brake calliper.

'Sir?' Lyle's smudged face peered up at him.

'Can I trust you to look after my wheels when I'm away?'

'You surely can, sir!' Lyle said eagerly.

'You certainly don't sound reluctant,' Garner remarked drily. 'All right. I'll leave you the keys whenever I'm not here. Take the Boss for a run if you want, but Lyle . . .'

'Sir?'

'One scratch, and you're history.'

Lyle grinned. 'I'll treat the Boss like my own, sir . . . only better.'

'See that you do.'

'Yessir!'

Lyle ducked back under the car.

5

Both Adderly and Garner were precisely on time for the briefing, though each had arrived independently.

For Adderly, it was a traumatic return.

Everything had gone beautifully. It had been a joy to play with the baby. The child had made precious few demands. He'd howled when he needed to be fed and changed, but that had virtually been it. In between takes, he'd been as content and happy as anyone could have wished for, and had slept when he needed to. Friends who had visited had said they'd never seen such an accommodating baby.

Things between him and Arlene had been great – until the last night. In the middle of lovemaking, she had suddenly begun to weep.

'Take it out!' she'd cried. '*Take it out!* It's all your fault. You put it in there and made me pregnant. You made me lose my baby!'

Shocked, he'd withdrawn from her and lain on his back staring up at the ceiling, while she had bunched herself into a protective ball and continued weeping. He'd had no idea how long he'd remained like that, listening to her, feeling the gluey dampness from within her on his inner thigh, all lust having unceremoniously vanished.

He'd tried to take her in his arms, to comfort her, but she had flinched from him. The baby had slept through it all.

He'd woken up in the early hours, to find Arlene's lips on his.

'I'm so sorry about last night,' she'd said, voice full of remorse.

But she'd been looking twitchy again. She hadn't wanted him to leave.

In order to spend as much time with her and the boy as possible, he'd opted for the latest MAC flight he could find *en route* to the Arizona base which would still enable him to arrive in time for the briefing. The flight west would get him back on the base a good half-hour early, local time.

'You're not the only pilot around,' she'd said. 'Why can't they let you off for a while?'

'It's my job, Arlene. I can't let someone else take my duty.'

'And what about your family? Don't you have a duty to us too?'

'Sure I do. This is all part of it. Arlene . . . you knew what I was when you married me.'

She had fallen silent, and he'd found himself wondering if he shouldn't pay another visit to the MO when he returned from the mission. Hours before, he had been enjoying the best sex with her since the new baby; then it had all changed. Back to square one. They had barely kissed when he'd said goodbye.

'It's because she doesn't want you to go back,' Nadine had told him quietly, out of Arlene's earshot. 'Give her the time, Nate. She'll come out of it. I know what I'm talking about. I've lost a baby too.'

He had stared at his mother-in-law. 'I never imagined . . .'

'Why should you? Arlene doesn't know.'

He had taken some small hope from that, but he was still very worried.

He now pushed these thoughts from his mind as footsteps tramped into the room. Both he and Garner came to attention.

'At ease, gentlemen!' ordered the familiar deep voice as Dempsey came up to position himself before them. 'Please resume your seats. Punctual,' he went on approvingly. 'Mr Garner.

I hear you've got yourself a classic Mustang. Been working on it?'

'Yes, sir.'

'Is it any good?'

'The best, sir. A Boss 429.'

'When you get back, I want a ride in that thing.'

Garner smiled. 'Consider your seat booked.'

'I do. And you, Mr Adderly. Did you enjoy your time with the family?'

'Yes, thank you, sir. And thanks for getting me the flights at such short notice.'

Dempsey's eyes studied him closely. 'Everything OK back there?'

'Yes, sir.'

'The question's a serious one, Captain. I want your mind very clear on this mission.'

'My mind *is* clear, sir.'

'Then we'd better begin.'

Dempsey had brought company. Major Carter stood to one side, legs slightly apart, hands behind his back.

The other person was a woman, also in a major's uniform. She was tall, with a finely chiselled face. Gleaming red hair, drawn tightly and secured in a bun at the back, showed beneath her air force hat. Hers was an athletic-looking body that gave an impression of latent and vibrant power. Her eyes, a strikingly bright green, were very hard to look away from. They demanded that you look at her.

She was, Garner thought, a beauty, and probably had a lot of trouble with men; mainly trying to keep out of their clutches. She had a body that made you want to sit on your hands, in case they betrayed you. He was equally certain she was no pushover. This was not a woman who took any crap from anyone, unless she chose to. He guessed her age at about the late twenties; which meant she was moving fast up the ranks. A real high-flyer.

'This is Major Hoag, gentlemen,' Dempsey was saying. 'Major Hoag is an Intelligence officer. She has relevant information about your mission. Listen very carefully to what she has to say. Major.' He stood aside to allow her to step forward.

A projector with a large screen had been set up next to the debriefing workstation. Next to the projector was a small table, and Major Hoag placed her briefcase on it. She then removed her hat and placed it carefully by the case. Now fully uncovered, the red hair was even more lustrous. She did not pat at it reassuringly. This woman had enough self-assurance for an entire squadron of ego-rich fighter jocks. She turned towards them, green eyes commanding their attention.

'I'm Shelley Hoag,' she began, introducing a note of informality, in a voice that was warm and friendly. 'My grandfather was Colonel Hoag, also in Intelligence. I make the point only because there is a connection with your mission. During the war in Korea, my grandfather was responsible for handling a very sensitive incident in 1951. As the world outside now knows, but only suspected during that war, the Soviet Union rotated whole squadrons of jets and their pilots to fight alongside the North Koreans, even ordering these pilots to pretend they were themselves North Koreans.

'Their aircraft all carried the NK insignia . . . all, that is, except for one unit. This was a special squadron, equipped with the very best of the MiG-15s, and ostensibly set up by a KGB general who appears to have had a very wide jurisdiction. It's job was intended to be the decimation of Allied aircraft, with special attention to the F-86 Sabre. For a while, they did just that. The pilots were all Second World War veterans, some of whom were aces. They were commanded by a woman.'

Major Hoag paused, her voice clearly indicating approval of a female appointment to command, as well as carrying an air of reproach. Her secondary message was that she felt there should be more female fighter pilots in the air force. Dempsey remained impassive, but Carter's face showed clearly what *he* thought of that idea.

Shelley Hoag glanced at each of the senior officers, the tiniest of smiles teasing at the corners of her mouth. She understood only too well precisely what Dempsey and Carter really thought.

'The special unit,' she went on, 'was unofficially called the Green Ringers. They seem to have had a kind of needle match with one particular US Air Force squadron. This was commanded by a Royal Air Force Squadron Leader, who was seconded to the USAF at the time. This unit flew F-86s, and was one of the most successful squadrons out there.

'It completely destroyed the Green Ringer squadron. The squadron commander himself shot down the Russian commander. Her body was recovered by our people. A very bizarre incident took place after the recovery. The RAF officer discovered that not only had he met her previously in Berlin, but they had actually danced together during the end-of-war celebrations.'

Her disclosures had them riveted. Even Carter, who'd never heard this before, could not prevent himself from being fascinated by the tale.

'Shit,' Garner said involuntarily.

The green eyes seemed to twinkle at him. 'Shit is right, Captain. My grandfather took charge of the body and had it shipped out. Years later, it came to our attention that not all members of that special unit had been killed. One pilot had ejected safely, but never returned to the Soviet Union.

'He was from one of the Asian Soviet republics and he stayed in North Korea, successfully passing himself off as a border Korean. He clearly had no intention of facing the wrath of Stalin all by himself, after the catastrophic failure of his squadron. It was a time for scapegoats, and I don't blame him. He is still alive, which is more than he could have expected had he gone back home. His sideways defection was our gain. Let us simply say he's been of use to us for many years.'

Major Hoag now turned to the projector and switched it on. Using a remote control, she brought a map up on the screen, showing the border region that covered North Korea, China and Russia. Each border was outlined in a different colour, so that the demarcation between the three countries was clearly visible. With the device, she drew a white circle about the area where the borders were closest to each other.

'This part of the world,' she said, 'is either going to be one of the most hotly contested pieces of real estate in the not too distant future, or it's going to be the basis of a new alliance. For the moment, we favour the alliance scenario.'

Dividing her attention between the screen and her audience, she continued, 'The world is supposed to have changed. We think not. North Korea and China are still communist countries and as for Russia . . . the recent elections have shown that old habits die very hard indeed.'

She clicked the remote and the area within the circle expanded to fill the entire screen. She clicked it once more and a small arrow appeared. Using the arrow, she first moved it along the North Korean border with China.

'From Musan,' she said, 'the border meanders and loops up here in the north-east, before doubling back southward, following this river here, all the way down to the Sea of Japan. For about twenty kilometres up from the coast, the border is with Russia. Then here, at Namjungsan, it splits – with the Russian

border now moving eastward as it goes north –
to create a forty-kilometre corridor to Nanhua
as part of China, before opening out from there
and into the rest of that country.

'According to our information, somewhere
within that three-country sector is a very special
site.' She turned from the screen to look at them.
'There are three possibilities: a nuclear facility,
a chemical weapons programme or . . . a secret
fighter base *dug into the mountains*, where pilots
from *all* three countries are being trained on
advanced fighters.

'I personally favour the last option. I believe
that something close to the alliance of the
Korean War may be taking shape again. Apart
from this airfield here, just inside the North
Korean border at Kyonhung, and this unnamed
one forty kilometres directly south, there are no
others in either country within that area, except
for a minor field south-east of Kraskino, Russia.
At least, none that we are currently aware of.
We have been unable to spot any aerial activity
from this mountain base, if it exists.' Using the
remote, Major Hoag drew a small square on
the map. 'Our information puts the most likely
location of the site within this box. We'd like
to know what's really in there.' She stopped,
and looked at the colonel.

'Thank you, Major,' Dempsey said.

She inclined her head slightly. 'Sir.'

'May I have the remote?'

'Yes, sir.' She handed it over, and moved to one side.

'Thank you.' Dempsey looked at Garner and Adderly. 'I think, gentlemen, you have begun to grasp the nature of the mission: a low-level reconnaissance. In effect, a ferret flight, to sniff out whatever they've got hidden in there. As Major Hoag has said, we don't *know* for sure; but if there's some kind of international fighter-pilot training facility in those mountains, we've got to plug that gap in our intelligence data. If that base does exist, it becomes a target *if and when* such a need arises.

'With the excitement going on down in the Taiwan Straits, we've got to know whether at some future date if Korea erupts again, or the Taiwan situation goes really hot, what kind of stuff we're going to be facing. According to the major, the news is that the very latest versions of the MiG-29 and the Su-27 are being flown by those pilots.'

Dempsey turned to the map on the screen. 'Take a good look at the topography. We cannot give you much in the way of suspected SAM sites, so any such information displayed will be speculative; but you can bet your shirt the area *will* be protected. Use every scrap of cover you can find, to hide yourselves from their radars. Ingress to target will be as low as you can hack it.'

He turned to face them, eyes seeming to drill into their very souls. 'Remember what I said about avoidance. We're not looking for a war, and we don't want a downed Eagle out there, gentlemen – and we certainly don't want captured aircrew. That would be very bad news indeed – for us and most particularly for you. Do not expect kind treatment if you are captured. If the worst comes to the worst, you will therefore make every effort to avoid being taken.

'If this doomsday scenario does occur, you must try to get the aircraft as close as possible to this point.' Dempsey pointed to a lake which was skirted by a railway line, not far from the coast. A road ran parallel to the rail line. 'A rescue mission will be on stand-by should there be a need.

'The Taiwan Straits party is good cover. Not only has it got attention focused down there, but Navy ships in the area around where you'll be going in will not arouse undue interest. It will appear to be just another muscle-flexing exercise, to guard our assets up that way. With the shadow-boxing going on down near Taiwan, a battle group on manoeuvres up here will be almost expected as par for the course. They would be more suspicious if there *wasn't* one. At this time they have no reason to suspect we have any knowledge of their little mountain hide-out.

'Our information is that there is no habitation in the area for several miles around. Don't take that for granted and, of course, there's always the risk of a patrol, particularly if the ether is humming with news of a damaged foreign aircraft looking for somewhere to set down. So use that road only if necessary, but knowing where it is will help with your bearings. If you have made it to the RV point, a helicopter will be waiting.

'If you're forced to walk a long way to the rendezvous, a chopper will come every day at a specific time, which you will be given before you take off from the forward base. If you arrive early, you must find a way to secure yourselves until the rescue chopper makes it. There will be special forces aboard a second helicopter, to give the rescue mission cover. Both choppers will be heavily armed, in order to sanitize the area, if need be.

'At no time will you engage in radio communication if you're down. Just leave your beacon on just long enough to let us know you're down OK. Thirty seconds. No more. We'll pick it up by satellite. Then get well away from the aircraft.

'Once your aircraft has been abandoned, charges placed in every piece of sensitive equipment aboard will detonate, ensuring nothing of use will be left for the enemy. If you eject, the detonators will go off once the seats are well clear. Your aircraft will carry no unit markings, and your names will have been removed from beneath the cockpit rim. This will be done in Japan, before you take off on the mission. You will, of course, be carrying handguns and enough ammo to see you through until the rescue. The hope is that you will not have to use them. Optimum result is that no rescue will become necessary.

'Rules of engagement: you will not attack *any* ground target. You will not attack any air target *unless* this is in self-defence. In short, you *wait* until he has launched at you. Even at that stage, it is better that you bug out. I know, I know, gentlemen. It's a tough break, but there it is. However, after he has initiated that first launch, he or any buddies he may have with him, are fair game. Use your initiative, but *always* remember: hang around only long enough to punch your way out of there.'

At last Dempsey paused. 'Questions?'

Garner and Adderly looked at each other, then looked at Dempsey. They shook their heads.

He turned to Shelley Hoag. 'Major?'

'I'm done here, sir.'

Dempsey again turned to Garner and Adderly. 'The mission is designated Organ Pipe, and your waypoint pattern will approximately follow the boundaries of the Organ Pipe cactus national monument, down on the Mexican border. You are Cactus One. The pattern is roughly kite-shaped. Position it so that the tail straddles the RV point. Modify that basic shape to your mission requirements, but remain *within* it. If for any reason you can't make the RV, we'll know the area within which to conduct a major search. Let's hope we won't have to, because by then the shit will really be *in* the fan.

'Clock's ticking as of now, gentlemen. Remain here and set up your waypoints. You will not be disturbed. You will take off at 14.00 hours for Alaska. Lancer and Hershon will accompany you, but will not know the mission. From

Alaska, both aircraft will stage to Japan. You will fly the mission from there. Thank you, gentlemen.'

While the colonel had been speaking, Major Hoag had picked up her hat and put it back on. She now picked up the briefcase and walked out, followed by Dempsey and Carter. Then the door to the room opened again, and she was standing in the doorway.

'Is it really a Boss Mustang?' she asked Garner. 'A 429?'

'It is.'

The green eyes smiled at him. 'I'd like to try it when the mission's done.'

'Then your seat's booked too.'

'I mean *drive* it.'

'It's a date.'

The eyes were speculative, and amused. 'A *date*?'

'A date. Take it or leave it, Major.'

'I'll take it.' She beamed at him and backed out of the door, closing it softly.

'That was quick work,' Adderly remarked lightly, introducing a note of friendliness between them. 'Your Boss Mustang must be bringing you luck.'

'She's quite a lady.'

'Careful. You'll make Arlene jealous.'

'Arlene's already got her man,' Garner said easily. 'You. And how is she?' he added.

'You really asking? Or making polite conversation?'

'I'm really asking.'

'She's OK.'

'Just OK?'

'She'd like to see you, Milt. She specifically asked me to invite you. I promised her I wouldn't take no for an answer.'

Garner fell silent.

'Look,' Adderly went on. 'I think it would help her if you did visit. Sometimes blood family can be too close to the problem. You know how she used to enjoy having you around. She feels as if you're making her pay for your beef with me. Don't do it for my sake. Do it for Arlene's. That's always assuming you really do care about her, and you're not just making polite talk.'

'That was a low blow, Nathan.'

'Yeah. It was, wasn't it?' Adderly did not sound repentant.

Garner passed a thoughtful hand across his eyes and said nothing. He looked as if he'd been boxed into a corner.

'We work well together in the air,' Adderly said, pressing home his advantage, 'but if you want another pilot when this mission is over, go right ahead. I won't stop you. Just remember, we used to be friends. I'd like it back that way. So would Arlene.'

'Then why didn't you trust me enough to tell me about that wonderful human being, old Nathan Adderly, the slave-owning ancestor whose name you carry?'

'Do you think it was *easy* for me? I would have told you eventually . . .'

'*Eventually?*'

'Milt . . . listen . . . throughout these United States we have sworn to defend, there must be . . . God knows how many families with a history like ours . . .'

'And it's still poisoning the damn country.'

'Don't you think I know that? Look. What say we concentrate on the mission and have a good long talk about this afterwards? Everything out in the open. As I've said, I want us to be friends again.'

Garner looked at his pilot for some moments. 'After the mission,' he agreed at last.

'OK. You got it.'

At exactly 14.00 hours, the two Echo Eagles lifted off in tight formation on the first leg of their flight, to the base near Anchorage, Alaska. They took off with a load of a centreline tank each, plus a full complement of four AIM-9L Sidewinder short-range heat-seeking missiles, and four AIM-120 AMRAAMS for longer-range kills.

Fully tanked up, the Echo Eagle had a ferry range of over 2700 miles; but they would be using the flight to do some air-to-air refuelling practice. For the stage from Alaska to Japan, they would need to refuel.

As Dempsey had indicated, Lancer and Hershon were totally unaware of the nature of the mission, but all mission data was ready for a fast and complete briefing, should the occasion arise. In the event of the first aircraft being compromised without first locating the secret base, the mission would be postponed. With the area on full alert as a result of the first Eagle's incursion, a second flight would be suicidal in the short term. But options were open.

Garner had programmed the entire mission waypoint data into the system, ready to be called up when needed. This started from the base in Japan. They would use separate data, copied to Lancer's aircraft, for the flight from Arizona to Japan. Everything that could be done to ensure a successful mission had been attended to. They had also double-checked their survival vests, ensuring that all was as it should be. An omission could mean the difference between life and death; between rescue and capture.

Garner ran through the list in his mind, as the Eagles climbed to high altitude for the fast transit to Anchorage: radio, mirror, flares, pencil flare gun, smoke, food, water bottle, fish hooks, knife, torch, strobe, pistol and ammo, and more. He would again double-check before take-off from the Alaskan base, and yet again from Japan, at the start of the mission proper. He knew Adderly would have done and would do the same, with his own kit. They were leaving nothing to chance.

He looked across to where Lancer's and Hershon's aircraft was keeping perfect station, and remembered Lancer's challenge.

'You guys may be kings of the walk,' Lancer had said as they had sauntered towards their waiting Echo Eagle, 'getting both Robert E. and killer, but you haven't come up against us. Reckon you can take us in a turning fight?'

Adderly had looked at him. 'This is a joke. Right?'

Garner had smiled, waiting for Lancer's reaction. Adderly could chew Lancer to pieces up there, any day of the week.

'Come on, guys,' Lancer had said. 'Not scared, are you?'

Garner had given Hershon a quick glance.

'Don't look at me,' Hershon had said, ducking out from under. 'I only fly with him.'

'When we get back,' Adderly had told Lancer, 'you're in for a sharp lesson. There will be weeping, and the gnashing of teeth.'

'Says who?'

'Says the man you can never beat, boy.'

Garner had given Hershon another surreptitious glance.

'Don't look at me,' Hershon had pleaded.

Garner smiled as he remembered. Lancer really should have known better.

Before leaving, Garner had also given Mason Lyle permission to look after the Mustang and to drive it, backing that up by giving the air policeman written authorization, just in case Lyle was stopped for any reason.

He relaxed in his seat as they settled out of the climb at 50,000 feet. Everything was done. The mission was on.

Let's get in, and get out quickly, he said to himself in his mind.

'You OK back there, Milt?' came Adderly's voice on the headphones.

'I'm fine.'

'This is it, huh?'

'It is.'

'In and out. Greased lightning.' Adderly was clearly having the same thoughts.

'Greased lightning,' Garner agreed.

After that, there was very little conversation between them. The aircraft flew on smoothly, all its systems fully operational, its technology working as it was meant to. Its crew, for the time being, had been relegated to the role of systems managers, watching like hawks to ensure that nothing went wrong or, if it did, to take swift remedial action. Highly trained and skilled individuals, they sat astride their potent steeds, marking the thin air with their passage.

Garner took a quick look at Lancer's and Hershon's aircraft. The Californian beach god was keeping faultless station.

About a thousand miles into the flight, they made a rendezvous with the KC-10 tanker at 20,000 feet above the Pacific, off the coast of Newport, Oregon.

'Anyone see a gas station around here?' Lancer quipped at the tanker aircraft.

'Be nice, sir,' the boom operator answered, 'or you'll go thirsty.' A woman's voice.

'I'm nice, I'm nice!'

Everyone could sense the operator grinning as she said, 'Then come on to mama for some refreshing JP4!'

Adderly had instructed Lancer to go first. The long boom, with its steerable fins close to the tip, extended as Lancer moved the Echo Eagle into position. Carefully, he eased forward, the aircraft weaving slightly in the tanker's wake. The KC-10's operator helped by steering the boom towards the fuel intake receptacle on the Eagle's left shoulder blister, next to the rear quarter of the engine intake's upper housing. The boom slid in, connected. Fuel rushed through the metallic umbilical cord at speed, giving the Eagle a generous drink.

Off to one side, Garner watched the process, checking out the wingman's aircraft as it drank. He knew that Hershon, in the back seat, would be eyes-out-of-cockpit, ready to warn Lancer of any impending danger. It was not unknown for customer and tanker to merge into an all-consuming fireball. All it needed was one bad mistake from either aircraft.

But everything went smoothly and Lancer had decoupled, and was banking the Eagle gracefully away.

Garner now checked out their own aircraft as Adderly swung into position. The boom came towards him, looking as if it was about to stab him between the eyes. Then it wavered slightly and clunked neatly into place, just past his left shoulder. The fuel pulsed through and soon they too were banking away, fully topped up.

'Nice to do business with you!' the operator called in parting. 'Y'all come again, now. Y'hear?'

'How about a phone number?' Lancer suggested.

'Never give ma number to strange men in airplanes. Out.' A giggle sounded before transmission was cut.

'Life's tough, Lancer,' Garner said.

'Looking forward to trashing you guys,' Lancer retorted.

'Dream on.'

Garner had selected Channel 81 on the Tacan. The right CRT was diplaying the main navigation format, with the steering bug on the compass rose showing five degrees off track. He compared that with the waypoint on the left-hand display. On the top right of the nav display, distance to the base showed forty-five nautical miles and was counting down.

'Come left three-three-zero . . .' he began. 'Now!'

'Roger. Three-three-zero.'

Adderly eased the Eagle on to the new heading. As if glued to them, Lancer's aircraft kept perfect station, matching the manoeuvre.

'Three-five miles to touchdown.'

'Roger. Three-five miles.'

Garner looked out upon the grey and white-streaked slopes of the snowy Alaskan peaks. Beautiful, he thought, but only if they stayed where they were. Still, it was a breathtaking sight.

Now that they'd descended in preparation for landing, clouds wisped past them. Despite the brightness of what was left of the day this far north, spring would be a lot colder than in Arizona; an average of 46° Fahrenheit during the day, to Arizona's 84°. It wouldn't do to go down among these mountains. Minimum temperatures would be well below zero.

But the Eagle flew smoothly on, with not the slightest hiccup in her systems.

The landing was carried out in formation.

The fighter break was made snappily over the runway and held as a tight pair, as they curved round on the downwind leg. Adderly throttled back to maintain 250 knots. Gear down, flaps down. Three greens above the red wheel, confirming gear down and locked. The little oblongs with their green lettering announcing 'NOSE', 'LEFT', 'RIGHT'.

'Gear down and locked,' he heard Garner say in further confirmation.

All was well.

He executed a descending turn, lining up nicely on the runway. They were now a mile out, and at 300 feet. Lancer was right there, keeping station.

Runway numbers centred on the HUD. One hundred and sixty knots now, descending. Air brake extended. Touchdown. Speed 130 and decreasing. Hold nose up. Big wing giving excellent aerodynamic braking. Ninety knots. Nose is down. Rolling, slowing down. Tap brakes. Slowing right down. Taxi to parking slot.

'Cheated death again,' Garner said.

'Yep. Don't know how I do it.'

6

They spent the night and took off again at 08.00 hours the following morning, for the stage to Japan. They made a rendezvous with another tanker over the Aleutians, and crossed the dateline while tanking. Making a dog-leg to avoid the Kamchatka Peninsula in far eastern Russia, they touched down at the forward base on the southern tip of the north Japanese island of Hokkaido. The high-cruise flight, including time out for tanking, had taken six hours. It was 09.00 hours the next day.

'West is east,' Lancer remarked as the four of them walked away from their aircraft to the ubiquitous little Volkswagen van that ferried crews around the base. 'We went west and, hey presto, we're in the east. Welcome to Japan. Who's for sushi?'

'Did you learn all that at school?' Garner said as they began to climb aboard the van.

'Oh ho!' Lancer said, unabashed. 'Who's a sourpuss?'

Garner shook his head pityingly.

When they were all in, the driver set off at seemingly breakneck speed.

'Hey!' Lancer called to the driver. 'You trying to kill us?'

'Sorry, sir!' the driver called back cheerfully. He didn't slow down.

Lancer looked aggrieved. 'I fly over miles of ocean in an Eagle for the privilege of being killed on the ground by a nut of an enlisted man? Do something, Captains,' he went on to Garner and Adderly. 'You're the senior men here.'

Garner and Adderly just looked at him. Garner then gave Hershon a long-suffering glance.

'I just fly with him,' Hershon said.

Once they'd been installed in the officers' club, Garner and Adderly decided to catch up on some sleep. Lancer decided he was not ready for sleep and persuaded Hershon to stay up with him. Neither crew would be going off the base until the mission was over. For Garner and Adderly, take-off on the mission was 02.00 hours.

The four men were not to see each other again.

* * *

A secure briefing room had been set aside for
Garner and Adderly, within which to make
final checks on their planning. They found
two surprises waiting.

'Gentlemen,' Colonel Dempsey said.

'Colonel!' they both exclaimed.

'And the major,' Garner added, looking
pleased. 'The Mustang's not over here, sir,'
he said to Shelley Hoag.

She smiled at him. 'Colonel Dempsey wanted
to be here for when you got back. I persuaded
him to take me along. I've also got some extra
information. Should the worst happen, our
contact will be at the RV to help get you
under cover.'

'Isn't he old for that kind of thing?' Adderly
commented sceptically. 'He must be what . . .
seventy? Eighty?'

'Sixty-eight. He's been doing plenty of mountain walking over the last forty years. He's a
lot younger than the Republican nominee, and
probably fitter than either of you.'

'Well,' Garner said. 'That puts us in our
place.'

'Your aircraft has been prepared,' Dempsey
cut in. 'To keep you as light as possible, the
centreline tank has been removed. When you
find the target, send the details via secure

datalink, and get the hell out of there. In case you're forced to turn and burn before you get out, there'll be a tanker waiting on station. You will rendezvous with the tanker on egress, 300 miles from the coast. Make sure you've got at least bingo fuel to get you there. So watch that fuel flow if you've got to engage in combat, or you'll be going for a swim.'

Bingo fuel state was their safety margin, enough to get them to the tanker with still sufficient left, in case they had to look around for it. There had been cases during the Gulf War of aircraft returning thirsty from their missions and either finding dried-out tankers, or missing their rendezvous points. Luckily, other tankers had come to their rescue.

This was a different situation. There would be just the one tanker. But even without the centreline tank, they would be carrying sufficient fuel for the mission, and still be able to make it back to base at bingo state; but that excluded fuel-consuming combat.

'We certainly don't want to swim,' Adderly said.

'Didn't think so.' Dempsey stared at them. 'Good luck, gentlemen.'

'Sir,' they both said.

Major Hoag hung around as the colonel

left. 'Not as tough as he likes to think, is he?' she began.

'What do you mean?' Garner asked.

'He tries not to show it, but he's not going to relax until you two are back.' She gave his arm a brief squeeze. 'Good luck. Both of you.'

She hurried out.

'"Good luck",' Adderly mimicked. '"Both of you". Notice that afterthought?'

'What afterthought?'

Adderly made a scoffing noise. '"What afterthought?" he says. She's after your balls. I mean that literally. That kind of woman is dangerous.'

'Bull.'

'Oh yeah? She doesn't want just a ride in your Mustang. She wants to *drive* it.'

'So?'

'You don't get it, do you?'

'So tell me.'

'That kind of woman likes to be on top . . .'

'I'm liking it already. She can ride my mustang anytime . . .'

'Forget your dick and where you'd like to put it. She's a control freak. You'll always be fighting her for control. Take my word for it. That one's grief on legs. Or have you forgotten what happened to you in New York?'

'I thought you said my lucky Mustang brought the sexy major to me. You've changed your mind about her so suddenly?'

'I haven't changed my mind. She's exactly what I expect her to be.'

Garner said nothing to that.

'Know what really hooks me about Arlene, even with our current problem?' Adderly went on. 'It's not just because she looks great, and it's not only because she's great at sex. She *needs* me, as much as I need her. That's what makes it work for me; for us. A woman doesn't need you, you're headed for trouble. Major Shelley Hoag doesn't need anybody. She's going places, and picks up little amusements along the way. But you already know about that, don't you? Remember New York?

'I don't know how far you're hoping to get with the major with the body to kill for; but a lover should also be a friend. You don't crap on a friend. That girl in New York was not your friend, even during schooldays. She crapped on you. Shelley Hoag's nobody's friend . . . 'cepting maybe her own. Perhaps you've got a thing about such women. Watch your six, buddy.'

'Finished?'

Adderly gave a worldly smile. 'Sure.'

'Let's get on with the planning,' Garner said.

'Sure.'

The darkness, speckled by the runway lights, was something insubstantial beyond the environs of the base. The Echo Eagle was at the threshold, engines spooling up to take-off thrust.

Garner looked about him and paused as his gaze fell upon the control tower. Both Dempsey and Shelley Hoag, he knew, were in there to watch their departure.

Was she really the single-minded power babe that Nathan Adderly had painted? He put Adderly's comments about her out of his mind. Time enough to consider them when they returned. He glanced down at the nav display. The time was 01.59.55 . . . 02.00.00.

'We're out of here,' came Adderly's voice, and the Eagle began to roll, accelerating in an enormous rush as the 'burners came on.

Then the nose was rising and almost immediately the main wheels left the runway. They were airborne, hurled forward on twin tongues of blue-white flame.

Adderly raised the wheels swiftly.

'Gear locked,' Garner confirmed.

'Roger. Gear locked.'

Adderly banked hard out of the circuit and settled on to the heading of the first waypoint, in a shallow climb. He cut the afterburners.

Garner had watched the map display rotate until it steadied, now moving as the aircraft position marker traversed its surface. He cross-checked with the waypoint display. All OK.

They would be covering the first 460 miles at high altitude. Any interested snooping radars and satellites would log just another standard flight from the many training missions of either Japanese or US aircraft. At 460 miles the Echo Eagle would head steeply for the lower levels until, at 300 feet, it would turn towards the target area.

With the FLIR on the HUD, they would go as low as they dared and head towards where Major Hoag's people had indicated the site was likely to be. Then it would be all up to how matters developed from then on.

Garner's mind went back to the moment when they had been just about to board the aircraft. Adderly had put a hand on his shoulder.

'We grab ourselves a coffee at the O-Club and have that talk when we get back.'

'We'll do it.'

'OK.'

Garner looked out at the night and wondered what was waiting for them out there.

'Waypoint two. Five miles. Three-zero-zero feet,' Garner announced.

'Two. Five miles. Three-zero-zero,' Adderly confirmed.

They were coming to the end of their steep descent and nearly at the required altitude. All active radar was on stand-by, closing down emissions. The passive radar warning receivers had remained silent. No one was currently taking overt interest in them. Waypoint three could change all that. By then, they would have intruded into potential enemy airspace.

'Waypoint two. Two-five seconds.' Garner watched as the remaining seconds counted down. 'Waypoint three, right two-nine-one degrees.'

'Two-nine-one.' Adderly took the Eagle into a gentle right turn. He watched as the compass numerals at the top of the HUD slid from right to left until the new course, marked by the small vertical line beneath it, was centred on the head-up display. 'On course.'

Garner thought he could sense his breathing

quickening slightly. This was it. They were about to poke their heads into the open jaws of the tiger. The trick would be to get them out again without having them bitten off.

'Going low,' Adderly said.

The Echo Eagle began to descend until it reached 100 feet. Adderly flew on at that altitude.

Garner had repeated the HUD display combined with the FLIR navigation overlay, on his left CRT. The infrared image showed him lots of water rushing past beneath them. He had done a quick radar scan while still well out, but nothing had shown in their path. The route he had chosen was so far devoid of shipping, and even if some radar post somewhere had managed to catch the fleeting sweep, it had been far too brief to allow any chance of pinpointing. In any case, they were now a long way from that last position.

'Waypoint three . . . ten miles,' he called. Then, 'Five, four, three, two, one . . . Waypoint four . . . two-eight-zero. Twenty miles.' He had modified the kite-shaped pattern of the waypoints, but had remained within the area covered by it, as he had been instructed by Dempsey.

'Two-eight-zero. Twenty.'

Adderly confirmed the change of course and put the Eagle into a steep left bank and on to the new heading. He stayed at 100 feet.

The twenty miles was soon covered.

'Waypoint four . . . three-zero seconds. Waypoint five . . . right, two-nine-six . . . thirty-five miles.'

'Two-nine-six. Three-five.'

'And here's the coast.' Garner had spoken in a hushed voice as they crossed into Russian territory. They flashed over several bodies on enclosed water. Nothing screamed on the radar warning. Even Bitching Betty seemed to be holding her breath.

Adderly had found a path through rising ground. They kept going. Sixteen miles later, they were into Chinese territory. Still nothing squawked at them. Then the convoluted border had them crossing the meandering river, and into North Korean airspace. Still nothing on the radar warner.

'Jesus,' Garner began softly. 'Are we going to get away with it?'

'It ain't over till the radar sings,' Adderly said drily.

They crossed the river again as it looped and were once more over the territory of the People's Republic of China, this time within the six-mile corridor bounded by North Korea and Russia.

The ground was rising quickly now and twice, Betty called out altitude warnings.

'Target ten miles,' Garner warned. 'I'll leave all systems on stand-by until the last moment. Somebody must have heard us by now, even if they haven't picked us up yet.'

They were not on 'burners, so there were no tell-tale plumes of fire to mark their passage.

'According to this enhanced map,' Garner continued, 'we've got a nice low-level run on approach, then everything turns into a wall. So watch it. We'll need a real fast pull-up to clear. I'll hit the systems on the pull-up. If this isn't a wild-goose chase, anything out there will show.'

'Roger that.'

'It's just too damn quiet,' Garner muttered. He searched the darkness about him, as if expecting to see fighter aircraft bearing down on them. 'I've got this horrible feeling of being watched by a million pairs of eyes.'

'Quit that. You're getting itchy.'

'Better itchy than sleeping our way into a trap.'

'That bad?'

'Listen ... my scalp wants to leave my

skull.' Garner searched the darkness once more.

'*Jesus!*' Adderly suddenly shouted and the Eagle was standing on its tail, 'burners coming on as it reached for altitude.

Several things were happening at once and it was a testament to both men's astonishingly quick reaction times that not only was disaster averted, but Garner had actually managed to trigger the systems just *before* the pull-up, as the aircraft hauled itself up to clear what looked, on the infrared, like a never-ending cliff face. Then they were over and heading rapidly down for the nearest valley.

Adderly killed the 'burners as they swooped for the welcoming valley.

'Sweet Jesus!' Adderly said, sounding very shaken. 'Did you see it?'

'I saw,' Garner replied, his own voice none too steady. 'That was a goddam big airplane. As big as our bird, I'm sure.'

'Where the hell did it come from?'

'Let's not worry about where it came from. There's another one and they're out there, and looking for us now – with maybe an extra buddy, or two.'

'That scalp of yours was right. They were waiting. Did you get anything?'

'Got it and sent it while you were trying not to commit suicide. Should be a good picture. I don't think they were waiting. I think we surprised the hell out of them. We were certainly not expected.'

'Dig whatever it was out of the memory. Let's see what we got.'

Garner called up the 'picture' that the radar-enhanced infrared sweep had taken in that terrifying moment. What they saw was astonishing.

'Jesus!' Adderly exclaimed softly when Garner had repeated it on one of the front cockpit displays.

What they had caught was an aircraft in the very act of taking off from what seemed like a huge hole in the mountain. There was a perfect overhead plan view of the aeroplane, clearly following the one that had nearly slammed into them.

'Shit,' Adderly said. 'I know an Su-27K when I see one. That's a mean fucking airplane. I'm not arguing with them. I'm taking the fuckers out.'

'I'm with you.'

The beautiful, flowing lines and canard foreplanes of the so-called 'Sea Flanker' stood out clearly.

'Well, we know the sexy major's information was right,' Garner went on. 'But Sea Flankers coming *out of a mountain*?'

'It makes sense. Those foreplanes make it manoeuvre even better. They've probably got to turn pretty tight once they've got off that mountain runway. Hell, it's a land-based aircraft carrier. Smart stuff. They've gone one better than the Swiss. Thank Shelley Hoag's mole. Satellites could look for years and never find it. Imagine, there could be others like it.'

'Nightmare time.'

Back at the forward base in Japan, both Dempsey and Shelley Hoag were having the same thoughts.

The 'picture' had been flashed, at the instant of its taking from the Eagle, up to the repositioned satellite, and sent by the satellite to a receiving unit in the States and to a waiting intelligence-gathering aircraft well out into international airspace, simultaneously. The intelligence-gathering Boeing had then relayed it to the room where Dempsey and Shelley Hoag were waiting.

They were staring at the same image that Garner and Adderly had been looking at.

'I'll be damned,' Dempsey said quietly. 'Will

you just look at that thing? Those boys are good.
Now just get the hell out, you guys,' he added
fervently. He turned to Shelley Hoag. 'Well,
Major . . . looks like your people were right.
This is not a good thing to see.'

'No, sir.'

'What do you make of it?'

She stared at the image on the screen before
turning to look at him. 'First, the airplane.
Su-27K. From what my department knows,
and adding that knowledge to this picture, I
would say we are looking at something that's
like a huge, land-based aircraft carrier. They
have tunnelled a large runway through that
mountain, wide enough to take three airplanes
in a loose V on take-off and maybe even on
landing. Like a carrier, you take off and land
in one direction. You're always into wind; but
better than an aircraft carrier or even ordinary
runways, there are no crosswinds strong enough
to cause problems.

'Almost immediately on landing, you're into
the tunnel. Out of sight quickly. On take-off,
you're in the tunnel until the wheels leave the
ground. Then you're over the lip at the end –
just like on a carrier – but with plenty of drop to
gain flying speed if you screw up. The Su-27K's
canards enable it to manoeuvre tightly and also

give it extra lift for such operations. I'm certain they'll have arrester wires in there for rapid stops, instead of the normal braking parachutes. With the hook and that big speed brake on the spine, stopping will be no problem.

'The airplane's sturdy landing gear enables it to use indifferent surfaces, so it can take off and land even on stony ground. This means they don't have to build a pool-table-smooth runway. Its engine intakes are protected by gridded debris guards, so even a rough runway will present no problems with foreign object damage. No ingested debris, no FOD. The tunnel runway is also practically weatherproof. No snow, ice or rainwater to worry about.

'The exposed parts are so short, it would be no trouble to keep them clear at all times; and importantly for spotting, very little heat traces for the infrared cameras on satellites or recce aircraft to pick up; which is why we needed that close look. They've probably got some surface cooling systems for the exposed sections of the runway, to keep infrared signatures down.

'They're also bound to have filtration systems to keep the fumes out. I'd say via long tunnels that exit the gases a long way from the base, and well camouflaged. They could also have all their administration, accommodation and engineering scattered within that mountain area, mostly underground. The Su-27K's folding wings would also enable them to store more airplanes in there, just like on a carrier. Sir, this could be the first of a proposed system of airfields. And they've got the best camouflage in the world. Nature.'

Dempsey was silent for long moments, impressed by her very extensive and detailed knowledge.

'This is a nightmare,' he said at last. 'If we ever get into a scenario where we've got to take those assets out, finding them first will be one hell of a job. Attacking them would be another nightmare. Hell, I could hold off a potentially overwhelming force with a wing of Eagles, SAM sites and triple-A saturating the area and, as a third line of defence, specialist combat troops to deter a ground assault. I'm certain whoever commands that unit has the same idea. You'd have to launch stand-off weapons *into* that hole in the mountain. That would not be easy. They've probably even got huge blast doors at each end.'

Major Hoag leaned against a table, and slowly crossed one glorious leg over the other.

'There's always another way, Colonel,' she said calmly, 'if we're in a bad shooting war and we can't seal off those bases, or neutralize them enough to make them inoperative.'

Dempsey looked at her. 'And that is?'

'Decapitate the whole damn mountain.'

Dempsey was staring at her now. 'Excuse me?'

Shelley Hoag allowed a tiny smile to play about her tempting lips, and said nothing.

'Nuke 'em, you mean?' Dempsey asked disbelievingly.

She still said nothing, but the smile continued to play about her mouth.

'Jesus, Major,' Dempsey said. 'You scare the shit out of me. You know that?'

'It is an idea, sir. And one that may have to be seriously looked at one day. Or perhaps the tunnel runway is the trend of the future. We'll all be burying our airfields.'

'And then we'll start – how did you put it? – *decapitating* mountains all over the goddam planet. We'll be burying our airfields all right,' Dempsey added drily. 'You'll be suggesting this idea to your superiors?'

'Yes, sir. All options must be reviewed.'

'Some advice from an old warrior, Major Hoag. Put that one back in cold storage. Bury *that* for good. The object of this exercise, I *hope*, is to let them know we're on to them, so that they'll think twice about constructing more of those underground airfields. They'll know we'll be keeping a close watch from now on, and that it's all going down in the target data. We're trying to prevent a potential war scenario here.'

'Bet the Taiwanese think differently.'

'We're not the Taiwanese, Major. That's a different ball game down in the Straits.'

'Yes, sir.'

Shelley Hoag didn't sound as if she thought it was. To her, it was all part of the same picture. The posturings in the Taiwan Straits were a few small brush strokes being added in a far corner of that picture. The mountain airfield was another in a different part of the same thing. One day, it would all come together. Decisions would have to be made.

'Right now,' the colonel said, 'I'm more worried about those boys getting the hell out of there.'

'So am I, sir,' she said. 'What response will we make if they do get brought down, sir?'

'Response? We don't want them brought down, Major. We don't want them captured and used in propaganda displays on TV, or forced to sign papers saying they're imperialist dogs and all that crap. We don't want Korean War, Version Two.'

'But if they are shot down?' she insisted.

'I'm sure you haven't forgotten our contingency plan. We rescue them. We do not respond.'

'Yes, sir.'

Dempsey looked at her warily. Jesus, he thought.

'Anything?' Adderly enquired.

'Nope,' Garner replied. 'Same answer as thirty seconds ago. Nothing on the warner. All our radars are off, so there's nothing for them to acquire. But they can hear us, and somebody must be talking to those guys we saw.'

He looked about him. This was not like most areas in the West, where there was always some residual glow from a city or town below, or even on the horizon. Even over the desert back in Arizona, something showed. But here, a hundred and fifty perilous feet above a strange landscape, there was no light showing anywhere.

'Look at it this way,' he went on. 'The longer we remain undetected, the closer to home we're getting. Waypoint seven. Three miles. Then it's zero-nine-five for waypoint eight . . . forty miles. Home stretch to the coast.'

'Roger. I . . .'

'*Launch! Launch!*' Garner bawled. 'We have a heat-seeker! Go for height, but leave the 'burners alone! I'm spoofing!' He cranked his head round. He could see a bright flame searing the darkness, coming from above. 'Holy shit. It's his infrared tracking ball and sight. That's how he acquired us. Must be. These guys are usually ground-controlled intercept and never work independently.'

'Well, he hasn't read that book,' Adderly grunted as he hauled the Eagle into a punishing avoidance manoeuvre.

Or he's disobeyed his GCI, Garner thought. Or he let one loose on spec. Whatever, we've still gotten ourselves a missile on our butts. This isn't the colonel, or the major out there. This is for real, and these guys are out to kill us!

The dark world, seen only in infrared, tumbled disorientatingly as Adderly did his stuff.

Then an ominous tone sounded.

'The goddam thing's got a lock on us!' Garner shouted. 'Get out of the fucker's way, Nate! Lose it!'

He fired off another decoy. A bright sunburst turned a patch of darkness into temporary day.

161

Adderly flung the big Eagle on to its back and plunged from the 10,000 feet he'd rapidly gained, towards the ground. He watched the AGL altitude on the infrared HUD as it counted down. There was a difference of 1000 feet between height above ground and above sea level. Many pilots had gone in, reading the wrong set of numerals. A thousand feet between life and death.

A valley opened up before him. He took the Eagle into it. Something bloomed brightly in the distance.

'There goes his missile,' Garner said with relief.

'All right,' Adderly said. 'We've obeyed the rules of engagement. I don't think this guy's going to let us get away without a fight. His buddy, or buddies, may already be trying to close the door on us. Let's kick ass if we want to get out of here.'

'You got it. Radars going on. Auto acquisition.'

'OKayyyy. Let's go to the party.'

Adderly hauled the Eagle into another steep climb, heading for altitude. Control the vertical before you go vertical, was the instructors' mantra; but there was no choice tonight. He needed some elbow room. The dive had given him plenty of energy, without need of the 'burners. He used that to convert to height.

Garner was making brief sweeps of the radar as the Eagle came over on to its back and began to drop its nose once more.

There!

'Got one!' he called. 'Got two!'

'Going to AIM-120,' Adderly said as he selected AMRAAMS.

Almost immediately, the targeting box appeared and began hunting. Then the seeker acquired. The box was solid. He began to manoeuvre to bring the box into the steering circle.

This would have to be quick. No time for fancy moves. Kill them and get out. Fast. Get him first before he manages to get another one off, forcing you to break your own lock, so as to manoeuvre out of his shot's killing envelope.

Range decreasing rapidly.

Shoot cue on. *Fire*.

Adderly pressed the release. The missile went off the rails in a blaze of fire that lit up the aircraft starkly, as it streaked towards the target.

See us for miles, Garner thought.

Then it was dark again as Adderly racked the Eagle into a diving spiral, to spoil any attempt by the opposing aircraft for another lock.

Would they get the kill? Garner wondered. Or was the other pilot, out there in the dark, already into his own ferocious avoidance manoeuvres? Was he jamming and spoofing like mad to escape being killed? Was he going to make it?

A flash in the distance.

A kill? Or had the missile expired uselessly on a decoy?

Major Konstantin Ilyich Udlov felt a deep sense of helpless frustration as he watched Captain Yeung die. The North Korean had disobeyed his advice and had not waited, and had paid the ultimate price for his haste.

Udlov had first heard Yeung's startled cry, followed by an excited rush of words. Yeung had reported that he'd nearly collided with another aircraft. At first, Udlov had thought the North Korean was still shaky from his first night take-off in the aircraft. He must have lost height rapidly, and had nearly gone into the trees far below the cliff face, Udlov had concluded.

Then twin plumes of flame had nearly scorched his own Su-27K, as he had followed Yeung into the air. The unknown aircraft had missed him but, experienced pilot though he was, the incident had left him temporarily shaken. It was then that he'd understood the reason for Yeung's sudden torrent of words.

But he'd recovered quickly. Who was the unauthorized maniac out there? He'd angrily demanded answers from those on the ground. There were no other friendly aircraft around, authorized or unauthorized, they'd told him. Then a message had come through of the noise of a low-flying aircraft coming up from the coast. It had not been challenged.

'*Why not?*' he'd barked furiously.

He would not have authorized the take-off if that piece of information had been received in time.

'We wanted to see where he was headed before shooting him down.'

Well, he's just shot down one of us, Udlov thought bitterly. And we know where he was headed.

Udlov was a tactics instructor, who knew the high value of patience. Had the excited Yeung not been so hasty with a missile release, they might have trapped the unknown aircraft in a classic pincer. Instead, the intruder had reacted very swiftly indeed. The pilot, whoever he was, was playing for keeps now. But how had he locked up Yeung so quickly? It had been a remarkably fast response.

Udlov could not know he was facing a two-man crew.

He did not call for another aircraft to be sent up. He'd been assured there was definitely just the one hostile target, and was certain he could handle it without the distraction of another insufficiently experienced pilot – even in a superb aircraft like the Su-27K – blundering about in the dark. He was determined to bring this intruder down by himself.

Then GCI began speaking to him.

Dempsey sat in the briefing room staring at the phone. He both wanted and dreaded to hear its ring. The news he wanted was that Cactus One was out. The other . . .

'Get some rest, sir,' Shelley Hoag advised. 'Why don't you? I'll wait here for the call.'

'Thank you, Major, but I think I'd better hang around. They should be on their way back, heading for the tanker rendezvous. We'll hear soon enough.'

'Yes, sir.'

But the colonel did not look at her. He was looking at the phone.

7

Major Udlov had a great liking for his Su-27K. He would even go so far as to say he loved it. It was, as far as he was concerned, a magnificent aircraft. It was potent, and the basis of this potency was the massive pair of Lyul'ka AL-31F afterburning turbofans that could hurl it through the air with astonishing speed. Its comparatively light weight, owed in no small measure to the incorporation of aluminium-lithium alloys in its construction, contributed greatly to this remarkable performance. It could turn very tightly indeed for such a big aeroplane, even at low altitudes and low speeds. It could also do its famous 'cobra' and snatch its nose round, while virtually appearing to be standing still in the air.

The first basic Su-27 had startled the West out of its complacency, just as the MiG-15 had done during the Korean War. It was a constant source of amusement to him, whenever the West thought it had discovered something new about the aircraft. Their interpretations of the uses for the various modifications they saw generated much hilarity among his fellow pilots back home in Russia. He thought it very ironic that here he now was, in one of the most accomplished variants of the Sukhoi, hunting out a Western intruder in the dark Korean sky.

He was in full agreement with the new and tentative friendship pact between the three countries, and the experiment of teaching the pilots of the two partners how to fly the advanced fighter. Many of them were still awed by its power, instead of revelling in it and making it work for them. Yeung had been one of those he would have marked down as being a top student; but the captain had made the worst mistake of a combat rookie. He had reacted hastily, underestimating his opponent. He had paid the inevitable price.

Udlov had no intention of making such an error, especially after what had just occurred. He was going to stalk this unknown enemy, prevent him from escaping, and shepherd him into the killing zone.

I'm going to drive him into coffin corner, Udlov decided grimly.

He would not use his radar, with its 240-kilometre long range for search, and 185-kilometre tracking range. This would alert the target and, in any case, he had little need of it. His infrared search and track system could spot a target from nearly 70 kilometres, and would give no warning. The missiles would be off the rails before the target aircraft even suspected he'd been tagged. The night was no hindrance.

GCI was speaking to him again, and directed him to where the intruder was heading.

Udlov opened the throttles but stayed out of 'burner to avoid visual detection. His present course would take him on a perfect intercept.

He was closing the door.

Then Udlov decided to reverse his earlier decision not to call up another aircraft. There was another of his students, who possessed an altogether more stable attitude: Captain Ling, of the People's Republic of China air force.

Though Ling did not appear to have the late Captain Yeung's flair, he was rather more than an efficient stick and rudder man. Ling was more precise in his flying than the flamboyant North Korean had been.

But he's just the kind of pilot I need right now,

Udlov thought, to help me trap this cunning bird out there.

He requested that Ling be sent aloft quickly.

In the tunnel, the alarm klaxons reverberated as the blast doors at each end were opened to the night. The runway lights were dimmed and all unnecessary illumination cut or switched to low-level red.

Captain Ling Chiu-Hua, secured within the enclosed world of his Su-27K's cockpit, waited for the slamming push of the catapult that would hurl him into the waiting darkness.

He moved the throttles smoothly to their full travel. The tunnel was suddenly bathed in a surreal glare of vivid light, as the 'burners speared their fire rearwards. He kept his head firmly, but without undue pressure, against the concave of the ejection seat's headrest as, with the familiar body-squeezing shove, the catapult hurled him into the night. He knew that even as he went into a steep accelerating climb, the blast doors were already being shut.

Ling felt proud to have been selected in the first place as a candidate for the new tri-national force and marvelled – as he continually did – at the ability of the aircraft to leap for altitude, even when pointing straight up. He cut the 'burners, not wanting to telegraph his position visually, and headed in the direction given by GCI.

He was also very proud of having been singled out by Major Udlov to aid him in this very important combat. Ling possessed utter respect for the Russian; as far as he was concerned, the major could do no wrong. He had listened avidly to every instruction Udlov had given him, throughout his conversion to this superb fighting aircraft. He had learned to stop being afraid of it, and to become at ease with its formidable capabilities. He had learned to look on the night as a friend, despite his limited experience. And it had all been due to the major's teaching and flying skills.

Ling's loyalty to Udlov was so great that it was touch-and-go whether he would back the Russian tactically, against the dictates of his own countrymen.

The American pilot – Ling was certain the intruder was American – would regret this incursion. Americans were always reckless. They thought they were omnipotent. He would show the imperialists that the price for such irresponsibility was very high indeed. This airspace violator and his imperialist compatriots would also one day discover to their cost – in the not too distant future – when the Korean comrades inevitably went on to reclaim the South, just how high it could be. It was only a matter of time. He was sure of it.

And he'd be right there in the thick of it with his fellow countrymen, supporting the comrades when the time came.

Ling banked the Sukhoi hard towards where Udlov was stalking the Eagle.

'We're in NK airspace,' Garner said as their track took them into North Korea.

He checked the threat display. It did not light up like a Christmas tree, and the audio warning had again relapsed into silence. It had been like that for some minutes now. He'd put the radars back on stand-by, to cut emissions.

'How's your scalp?' Adderly enquired.

'Still trying to leave my skull, and I've got an itch between my shoulder blades. They're still out there. One, two . . . who knows how many. We're definitely being stalked, even though there's no radar warning.'

'Infrared?'

'That's the baby. It's infrared search-and-track time. He, or they, are hunting us down with their night torch. If we got the other guy, there's maybe just one of them now and he'll be mean as hell. He wants our butts. We're going to have to be real fast and slick to get him first. We're going nowhere till we do.'

Though they were still heading in the general direction of the next waypoint, Adderly frequently altered course, never travelling on the same heading for long, and keeping as low as he dared.

'OK,' Adderly said. 'I'm going to try something. We're not going to wait for him to rope us, so let's hit him with the unexpected. I've got AIM-120 selected, and I'm going to give him two to play with. He should have a real party trying to dance the night away with those two babies after his ass. Meanwhile, we hightail it out of here. If he survives, we'll be well out to sea. Too late for him to come looking.'

'Sounds good to me. How do we do it?'

'We've been changing course all the time, so if GCI's been trying to guide him to us they can't be using radar, or we'd have known it . . .'

Then the radar warner clamoured for attention in his headphones. He threw the Eagle into a violent series of manoeuvres to break the scan, while its auto jammers went to work. The noise stopped. The probing radar no longer probed.

'You were saying?' Garner remarked drily. 'That was just long enough to set him on our tail. But they're not sure if we've got anti-radar missiles, so they've shut down pretty quick.'

'So he knows where we are at this time . . . or *thinks* he knows. OK. Here's the deal. I believe he may be in trail now, trying to sneak up for a close kill. It could be tricky, but I'm going for a sudden reversal. Head shot, if he's behind us. Get ready to hit the radars. If he's really there, we'll have him before he can use his gizmo. OK?'

'I'm ready to roll. I also have a thought.'

'Will I like it?'

'You might not.'

'Shoot.'

'What if,' Garner began, 'he's called up another buddy to replace the one we may just have splashed? What if there's a bunch of them out there?'

'It's a thought to give us nightmares. But that's the deck we've got, and we play the cards as they've been dealt. So we'd better get the sucker, and quick.'

'No complaints from me. You have full auto-acquisition.'

'Let's do it.'

Adderly suddenly pulled the Echo Eagle into a hard and tight turn, reversing on to a reciprocal heading. He was careful not to light the 'burners.

At the instant of the turn, Garner had used the side controllers to give Adderly the radars.

On the HUD, Adderly saw the targeting box come on, hunt briefly, then fix itself on the upper-left quadrant of the head-up display. He needed only a slight adjustment to ease the Eagle round until he got the box nicely into the missile steering circle. Almost immediately, he got the shoot cue.

He fired. Twice.

The night was lit doubly bright, as the two AIM-120s flashed off the rails and streaked into the far darkness.

'*Let's get the hell out of here!*' Adderly rasped, hauling the aircraft tightly round, to head for the waypoint.

Though they were rushing away at high speed, he desperately wanted to light the 'burners, so that they could extend the distance travelled at an even greater velocity. He disciplined himself not to push the throttles that much further, in order to demand full afterburning thrust. They would be lighting up the night for every heat-seeking SAM in the area. Not a smart move.

Garner had turned off the radar as soon as the missiles had gone. Now, as the infrared image of the HUD on his CRT whirled again, he glanced over at the waypoint display. He was very gratified to note that they were only six miles from the ground RV. He felt a great relief. They wouldn't be needing it.

The bogey would have his hands full by now, trying to disentangle himself from a pair of implacable AMRAAMS after his blood. They were going to make it home after all. The hope was that there was not a third bogey out there.

'Five miles to waypoint,' he announced.

'Roger. Five.'

Udlov felt sick. When he'd seen the pair of bright stars suddenly lighting up the sky, he knew instantly what had happened. The other pilot had correctly arrived at the conclusion that as his radar warning systems had been so conspicuously silent, he was being tracked by infrared. When the ground control had scanned for a position update, he had also correctly worked out what was happening. Although not certain of how many adversaries he faced, the intruder had done that most potent thing in combat: the unexpected.

Even as he watched the bright stars hurtling toward him, Udlov felt a chagrined admiration for the other pilot. He leaves me to cope with his missiles while he escapes, he reflected.

Udlov was already furiously ejecting decoys and heading earthwards to drag the missiles into a position where their great speed would force them into collision with the ground, when they tried to turn to follow him. Countermeasures would also make life very difficult for them.

One missile veered off, chasing a decoy. The other came on inexorably.

Udlov felt the sweat pop from his brow, making the helmet feel damp as he tried to evade the second missile. He flung the big, agile aircraft into seemingly impossible manoeuvres.

He had again gone for height, not wanting to make a terminal acquaintance with the ground.

The missile was still following.

The unknown pilot had been smart. Assuming that another adversary could be on the scene, he'd taken drastic action to lessen the odds as quickly as possible. No adversary remaining, and he was OK. Another, and it was still down to one-on-one.

'A smart move,' Udlov grunted as he continued to throw the big fighter into a furious series of evasive manoeuvres. 'Bastard!'

Ling was on his own now and at this rate

would probably be making a rapid exit. The Chinese pilot's chances of continuing survival did not look at all good.

Udlov swore at the missile, and at the American pilot who had fired it. Then he realized that unless he wanted to be roasted, it was time to get out.

'*He's getting away!*' he yelled at GCI. '*Ejecting! Ejecting!*'

He grabbed at the double-looped red handle between his knees and gave it a firm pull.

He ejected cleanly.

As he left the aircraft, he was aware of the rapid passage of something very hot. Fractions of a second later the missile's fire curved to the left and a violent sunburst smeared itself against the backdrop of the night, as it hit the abandoned aircraft. He'd got out just in time.

He would live to fight another day.

He experienced a feeling of sour pleasure as he floated towards the treetops. The SAMs had held back while the first two Sukhois were in the air, not wanting to hit them by mistake. Now they would be after the intruder with a vengeance. They would be less restrained, even with Ling around.

'Hope they get you, you bastard!' he said

in his native tongue, and cursed the unknown pilot again.

It was now up to Ling, and the SAMs.

Continuing down in the darkness, Udlov felt even less secure about Ling's chances. Despite his undoubtedly growing skills, the Chinese was still a long way from being independently capable of handling a fight like this; he still needed the guiding hand of a combat leader. Now out there on his own, he might as well be trapped in a darkened room with a vengeful cobra.

Udlov found that he now regretted having called out his pupil. He had sent the young pilot to certain death.

'Think we got him?' asked Adderly.

'He's either the best damn dodger there is with *two* 120s on his tail,' Garner replied, 'or he's toast. At least his airplane is. He could have got out, if he didn't leave it too late. Waypoint three miles.'

'Three miles.'

'Uh oh!' Garner said.

'What? *What?* Speak to me!'

'More company. Definitely more company.'

'*Goddamit!*'

'He must have called up another buddy, after

all. Best assume it's another of those hot Su-27K ships. But this guy's not as good. He's all over the radar warner. One-three-zero at thirty miles. He's too keen.'

'Then let's sock the dude in the teeth before he launches at us, and get out of here. I'm getting homesick.'

'You got it,' Garner said. 'He's now at two-three-nine, and still playing with his radar. I don't get it. He might as well say come and get me. He's still at thirty miles. Someone should have warned you about that radar, boy,' he added to the Sukhoi pilot.

'If he's not as good,' Adderly said tentatively, 'you reckon we can get him with the same trick?'

'Don't see why not. He's probably still in shock from watching the lead go down, and is wondering what the hell happened. I hope.'

'Perhaps we just splashed another rookie and it's the sharp one still out there, trying to sucker *us*.'

'Maybe,' Garner conceded, 'but I wouldn't go to the bookie's with it. The other guy might have tried that trick if the *two* of them were still out there, getting his wingman to corral us with the radar while he sneaked in for an infrared shoot. I think that's what they planned. I think we just ruined their day.'

'OK. We'll go with that.'

Ling was indeed in a state of shock.

Major Udlov shot down!

He didn't want to believe it. Even if he'd chosen to ignore the shocking news that had been relayed by GCI, he could not deny the evidence of his own eyes. He'd seen the brilliant flaring in the night, twelve kilometres away from his last position. He hoped the major had managed to escape injury. He had not picked up the Russian's eject cry, but GCI had given him as detailed a picture of the incident as they could. The only cheering aspect of the whole thing was the fact that the major appeared to have ejected cleanly.

Ling heard himself breathing deeply in his mask as he manoeuvred for a missile shot. He tightened his lips. This intruder was not going to get away with such impertinence. First Yeung, now Udlov.

It was time to collect from the American.

The missile warner was going crazy again.

'*Launch!*' Garner called. 'We've got a radar sniffer incoming, and it's got our names on it!'

'Too soon,' Adderly grunted, then groaned against the sudden onset of G-forces as he pulled the Eagle into a punishing turn, to reverse direction. 'He should have . . . waited a mite . . . longer. Lock not solid.'

They were now head on to the incoming missile.

Garner knew it was going to be close, but calmly set up the radar for auto-acquisition as Adderly manoeuvred for an AMRAAM shot. He watched the targeting box on the HUD repeater, watched as the missile seeker hunted then stabilized on the box; watched as Adderly manoeuvred so that the symbols drifted into the steering circle; saw the shoot cue come on; saw the sunburst in the night as the missile hurled itself off the rails to scar the darkness with its fiery wake.

Then the unseen world was again tumbling as Adderly threw the Echo Eagle into another set of frantic gyrations, as he fought to escape the impending terminal clutches of the radar homer that was seeking them out.

And all the while, the warning of the incoming missile filled their headphones.

Ling was occupied with his own avoidance manoeuvres.

At the moment that he'd launched his missile, his own warners had bayed at him. As he tried to escape the American missile, he thought grimly that both aircraft were now totally defensive, both so occupied with trying not to get shot down that neither could find the time to continue the attack.

And meanwhile, Ling thought furiously, he's getting away!

That pilot out there was very good. He hadn't wasted any time. Even within the barest of windows of opportunity, the speed of his reactions had enabled him to make certain of his lock, before missile release.

The American missile seemed implacable.

Ling threw the Su-27K into the series of manoeuvres he'd so assiduously learned from Major Udlov, breathing hard against the forces that mercilessly squeezed at him, but remaining calm throughout. He wasn't going to panic. The major had warned him about panic.

'Panic is a win for the enemy,' he remembered the major saying bluntly. 'Your tactical thinking is gone. You might as well fly straight and level, and give him the kill. Always think, *then* react. Do this so swiftly that it merges to become a single act. Thinking and reaction *must* be a seamless join.

Don't react and then think. By that time, you're dead.'

Ling heard the words pounding in his mind as he too fought to avoid the flaming nemesis that reached for him. He wondered whether he'd achieved a decent lock on the intruder. He hoped so. It would make up for Yeung and the major. It would be good to land with that kill to his credit.

But first, he had to get away from this determined missile.

'It's still with us!' Garner said, as calmly as he could. 'What was that about a solid lock?'

'So it didn't hear me,' Adderly grunted. 'What do you want? Miracles?'

'That would help.'

'OK. One miracle coming up.'

Adderly flung the Eagle on to its back and headed earthwards.

On the infrared display, Garner watched the image of some very ugly high ground reaching for them. He said nothing. Adderly knew what he was doing.

He'd better, he thought, staring at the image.

Then the terrifying image was receding and his body felt as if it wanted to fuse into the seat, as the Eagle was again reaching for the upper levels in a steep climb.

As the G-forces faded with seeming reluctance, Garner looked over his left shoulder and saw a flaring far below. The missile had been too close to the ground when it had tried to turn to follow them, and had impacted.

He shut his eyes briefly, sensing a great relief.

'Good enough for a miracle?' Adderly was saying.

'Give the man a nickel. Can we go home now?'

'Took the words right out of my mouth.'

I'm not going to get away, Ling thought clinically.

The American missile was still with him, trailing him with a single-mindedness that made him feel the thing had a mind of its own. It was as if the seeker head had become sentient and knew every manoeuvre he was capable of executing, *before* he went into them. It even ignored the decoys.

Surely it would run out of fuel soon?

Time seemed to stretch for ever. The missile appeared to be infernally happy to follow him for just as long.

I've got to do something!

Following Udlov's diktat of thinking and reacting seamlessly, Ling chopped the throttles and hauled the Sukhoi's nose into the vertical. The aircraft lost speed rapidly.

Without looking, he knew the missile was hurtling inexorably towards him, now in a flat trajectory. In his fevered mind he imagined he could hear it yelp for joy, knowing it had him cornered. The impact, he reasoned, would be at the precise point where the top of his head now was.

Please, please.

He waited, as the aircraft seemed to hang in the air as speed bled off and gravity began to take over.

Please, please.

Then the Su-27K seemed to drop like a stone, tail first.

A cone of fire hurtled past, several metres above as the missile punched through the space where the aircraft had been. But it was not to be thwarted. It began curving round, hunting out the prey that had dared to fool it.

Ling's immediate problem now was loss of both energy and control. His manoeuvre had been one of inspired desperation. Had the opposing aircraft been in the vicinity, letting

186

himself hang in the air like that would have been suicidal. A fat target going nowhere. But against the missile, it had proved to be a life-saver, if only somewhat temporary. But any extra time was a bonus; a chance to get away.

The missile was coming back.

Ling shoved the throttles forward as he fell. Power returned smoothly. Power brought flying speed. He rolled the Suhkoi into a ninety-degree bank and hauled into a turn that would force the missile to alter course, as it tried to reacquire him.

It came close. Then as if fed up with being continually balked, it exploded.

What sounded like a shower of hail rattled against the aircraft. It jolted severely, like a horse that had been jabbed by viciously applied spurs. It shuddered, seemed to shake itself as if brushing off the blow, and flew on.

But damage had been done. Power on one engine was falling rapidly. But there seemed to be no further damage. Ling was astonished to find he was still alive. There seemed to be a pool of sweat encasing his face, as he silently thanked the Fates for his good fortune.

He forced himself not to take deep gulps of oxygen as he did a swift check of his systems. The left engine appeared to be the only truly serious damage, but with it, some systems would eventually go.

Even so, he would make it back. He called the base to warn them he was damaged and coming in.

'Glad we got that bozo off our backs,' Adderly said. 'Man, I could use some coffee.'

'I could use something. It's got oak leaves on its shoulders.'

Adderly gave a resigned chuckle. 'You're not thinking of the sexy major, are you? After all I said? Some people just like living dangerously.'

'Have you *seen* that body? I'm not talking about a life-long commitment here. I know her game.'

'Don't fool yourself. When you *think* you know, that's when she'll throw you a big curve.'

'Hey . . . it's just a little rock 'n' roll. No big deal.' Even as he'd been talking, Garner was moving his head around, checking the night about him. 'Hold.'

The tenseness in his voice made Adderly say, 'What? What?'

'Thought I saw something flash way over at three o'clock. Low . . . *shit! Break right! Break right! SAM launch!*'

The flash had turned into a long stream of flame, and it was headed towards them. There had been no radar warning, so it was a heat-seeker, probably launched willy-nilly across their path in the hope of a kill.

Garner had begun his countermeasures even as Adderly again threw the Eagle into a series of avoidance turns.

'We must have got that third 27,' he said between grunts to Adderly as the G-forces came pressing at him intermittently, in response to the hard turns the aircraft was making. 'Or damaged him enough to send him back to his carrier in the mountain. So they've woken up the SAMs. Shit, shit, *shit!*'

The surface-to-air missile consumed itself violently in one of the flares from the Eagle.

'OK,' Adderly said, relaxing slightly. 'That's gone. Any more?'

'None so far ... *Launch! Launch! Six o'clock!* Jesus! Those bastards want our hides real bad.'

The radar warning went crazy. Bitching Betty joined it. The ECM systems went into their routines, and Adderly again did his daredevil stuff, keeping a sharp eye on the threat display. Again they managed to evade the missile. This one tried to follow the reflecting decoy, and went back towards the ground.

They were now four miles away from the waypoint.

'I think they're trying to herd us back,' Garner said grimly.

'No way,' Adderly said, and returned to course.

Garner was right about the intentions of those on the ground.

'*Launch! Launch!*' he called yet again. 'Two! Six o'clock and nine o'clock. These dudes are really after a kill tonight. Find a valley. Get away from the waypoint!'

For a third time the Eagle was flung about and the countermeasures went to work in an effort to deny the missiles their kill.

Adderly found a valley in which to temporarily hide. One missile followed, but took the turn into the valley too wide, and slammed into the opposite slope. The other seemed to have disappeared.

'We've got to get out of here,' Garner said, 'or we'll hit bingo fuel long before we make it to the tanker.'

They both knew that the combat manoeuvring had gone on for much longer than had been anticipated. If they didn't get away soon, they would be going for a swim. They tried to put the thought of being shot down out of their minds and concentrated on making their escape.

Garner was running the map through, looking for a route out. Mindful of the colonel's remarks about remaining within the kite-shaped pattern, he quickly set up new waypoints that would take them back to the egress point, but from a new direction that still gave them ground cover.

'New waypoints on your screen,' he said to Adderly. 'Old four is now eight. New four two-seven-zero at five miles. We should have the fuel if nothing else happens.'

'Roger,' Adderly confirmed.

They went through waypoints five, six and seven without any more attention from the SAMs.

'Nice going,' Adderly said. 'Looks like they lost us.'

'Don't bring out the champagne yet,' Garner cautioned. Waypoint eight . . . one-six-five . . . ten miles.'

'One-six-five. Ten.'

They were again approaching the ground RV point. The coast was just a little way ahead, and then the open sea.

*　　*　　*

Ling had shut down the damaged engine to lessen the risk of an in-flight fire. Hook down, wheels down, flaps down, ailerons drooping. He gingerly made a long, straight approach to the runway, holding the aircraft steady as it descended.

Though generally blacked out, they had put on the red horizontal lights that marked out the threshold of the section of the runway that was outside the tunnel.

His approach was steady, his speed good. He needed only the slightest of corrections on the rudder, in order to neutralize the natural tendency of the good engine to swing the aircraft slightly. There was no crosswind to give him extra trouble.

Then the almost sedate approach gave the impression of speeding up suddenly, as he got closer. He kept his nerve. If he panicked and jerked at the controls, the aircraft would swing or rise, and he'd be ploughing into the mountain itself.

He brought the Sukhoi steadily down. The wheels hit the runway, just ahead of the lights. The hook squealed as it scraped along then grabbed one of the four arrester cables. The Su-27K was jerked to an abrupt halt.

Ling quickly shut down the engine and

allowed himself a sigh of relief. He was down! He'd made it.

He was still alive.

The squad of soldiers had been told to look out for a foreign aircraft crashing but they'd neither seen nor heard anything. They were working their way in the dark, down a steep incline which was about fifteen miles from the ground RV point as the crow flew, but was a good thirty or more on foot, over rough terrain. If they were heading there, it would take them at the very least until the next night to make it. But they weren't headed there.

At least, not yet.

They came into a tiny clearing. Suddenly, they paused, listening. There was a sound; definitely the sound of an aircraft.

The squad leader shouted to one of the men to make his man-portable SAM launcher ready. It was a Chinese-made version of the old Soviet Strela, in use from the days of the Vietnam War, but still very effective. It even possessed a filtering capability, allowing the seeker to screen out flares that might be released as decoys, and still home in on the target aircraft.

The man worked quickly. Another soldier helped him load the plastic tube with the heat-seeking missile. He brought the launcher to his shoulder, and waited. He had no idea what he would be aiming at and judged the target by sound.

The launcher had an open sight only, which was of little use to him in the dark. But his hearing was acute, and he aimed where he thought the sound was coming from. However, a red light would come on in the sight when the infrared seeker was energized, and would change to green when it had achieved lock-on. All he then had to do was squeeze the trigger in the pistol grip.

As the sound grew louder, the soldier saw the red light come on. He waited patiently for the green; and it came. He fired, still without seeing his target.

The missile shot out of the tube, propelled by its booster motor, then when it was about twenty feet away the sustainer ignited, hurling the missile towards its target. Without this two-stage system, operators of that particular missile launcher would be toasted by their own weapon.

The squad watched as their missile flew.

*　　*　　*

'*Launch!*' Garner bawled in his mask. 'Six o'clock! Shit, shit, shit! Another heat-seeker! Where did *he* come from?'

Once again, he began countering the missile, feeding it the searingly hot flares, while Adderly threw the Eagle into punishing manoeuvres.

The missile came on.

'It's not taking the flares!' Garner said. 'Damn!'

He fed it some more. Adderly pulled out all the stops.

The missile followed.

'Shit,' Garner said. 'This thing looks like it's got our names on it.'

He kept turning his head, hunting out the missile's flaming plume, as Adderly used every move he knew in an attempt to beat the slavering fire on their tail.

Still the missile came on.

'Man, this is . . .' Garner began.

Then the missile exploded.

It didn't actually hit the aircraft, but it was close enough to do considerable damage. Its dying pieces ripped through the Eagle, most going through the front cockpit and the engines. Miraculously, the canopy was intact, as was the rear cockpit. Many systems remained on-line, and there was no fire. Yet. But the master caution was blinking like mad, and the warning tone was going. Bitching Betty added to the fun.

Garner did a rapid check of his systems.

The double row of the twenty-six lights of the aircraft systems warning panel, across the top of the two main CRTs, had begun to come on immediately after the missile explosion. But now, red lights started appearing in the group of eight on the left of the master caution light and, on the right, more captions were winking on.

The Eagle had pitched upwards, as if it had really felt the pain of the near impact.

Garner was unhurt. 'You OK?' he called to Adderly.

There was a long pause.

'*Nathan!* You OK? Talk to me!'

At last Adderly said, 'Take control.'

'*What?*'

'Right arm . . . right arm's useless. Take . . . take control.'

Jesus! Garner thought.

But he did not argue, and immediately assumed control of the aircraft and brought it back to level flight, roughly on course. He was no fighter jock, but he was sure he could fly it back to base. The problem was, there was not enough fuel to make it all the way back to Japan. And certainly, there was no way he could tank *at night*, without turning both their aircraft and the tanker into a fireball.

It looked like a swim, after all. Time to let them know. He dialled up the guard channel.

'Cactus One to Organ Pipe ... *mayday, mayday, mayday*. Cactus One to Organ Pipe ... *mayday, mayday, mayday*.'

No one replied.

'Cactus One to Organ Pipe ... *mayday, mayday, mayday* ...'

Still no response.

The warning panel had the story. All comms were out.

Great.

Two of his screens went blank and stared back at him like socketless eyes. The aircraft began to shake violently and he was having difficulty keeping it steady. It felt ready to roll over at any moment. A coarse rumble told him the engines were no longer happy. Engine RPM was dropping alarmingly. He worried about fire, every flyer's nightmare. Remarkably, the infrared HUD was still working and it was repeated on his left-hand display.

They were low enough for him to see that they were currently above reasonably open ground, and their heading showed they were still pointing the right way.

It was time to leave while he could still see roughly where they were, and the aircraft was still in level flight.

'Nathan! Can you hear me?' Garner spoke rapidly, urgently.

'Yes . . . yes . . .'

He sounded very weak, Garner thought anxiously.

'Nathan . . . we've got some bad ju-ju here. We're losing fuel, RPM's tumbling, radio's down, and the systems are going off-line. We're not going to make it. We're going to have to eject. I'm moving to aft initiate. You got that?'

'Yes . . .'

'All right. Here we go!'

They left the Eagle cleanly. It flew steadily in the dark for a good thirty seconds, then a vivid brightness lit up the night as it exploded. Secondary explosions followed.

'They'll have seen that for miles,' Garner said to himself as he floated down.

He hoped Adderly had made it without further injury. Ejection was not always the end of your problems, even over friendly territory.

By the time he'd landed, his eyes had adjusted themselves to the gloom. He came down just a few yards from the road that Dempsey had told them about. He quickly got free of his chute, then rolled it and hid it with his helmet as best he could. He kept on his G-suit and survival vest. After activating his beacon for the length of time specified by the colonel, he went to look for Adderly.

About five minutes later, he found him. Adderly had landed at the edge of the lake. His chute was in the water, with Adderly himself still attached to it, but his body was actually on dry land.

Before he risked touching him, Garner wanted to be certain there were no spinal injuries from the ejection.

'Nathan,' he began. 'Can you talk? Can you move?'

Adderly groaned softly. 'If . . . you're worried . . . about my back . . . it's OK. My arm . . . and my left ankle . . . are not so hot.'

Relieved there were no spinal problems, Garner began to work quickly to free his pilot from the chute, then eased away from the edge. He toyed with the idea of hauling the chute out, but it had filled with water. Then, even as he watched, its amorphous form began to disappear. It was sinking. He wondered where their seats had landed. Any troops within a thirty-mile radius might well stumble across those tell-tales within the next hours, and that would sharply focus the area of search, as they hunted for the users of those seats.

We've got to make it to the RV, he thought urgently.

Garner found that he could now see appreciably well, but knew it would take another thirty minutes or so before he acquired full night vision. He returned his attention to Adderly, whose injuries he could not yet examine properly, but whose right arm felt strange. Adderly had somehow managed to remove his helmet, for it was next to his good arm.

Expecting that the pilot would be suffering from some degree of shock because of his injuries, Garner began to gently check by feel. The facial skin was not cold or damp, pulse was strong, and breathing was regular. He couldn't check the eyes, but as far as shock was concerned, Adderly seemed to be OK for the moment.

'We've got to get out of here, Nathan,' he said. 'I don't know what other injuries you may have, but we're kind of exposed if we stay. I've got to move you. We'll find a hide-out, then I'll check you out with my torch. I've already sent the signal, so they'll know we're down. But we'll have to move during the night to get as close to the RV as we can. It's only about four miles from here, along this road. All we've got to do is follow it.'

He glanced along the road in both directions. There was not even a pinprick of light.

'We're in luck,' he continued. 'It doesn't look as if this road is the busiest in the world. But that can easily change. This may not be a car-owning democracy, but it's got plenty of soldiers. Soldiers mean military traffic. Come daylight, we go into the bush. Can you walk?'

'I . . . think so . . .'

'OK. Let's have a try.'

'Arrggh!'

'Sorry, sorry . . .'

'It's not you. It's the ankle. I don't think it's broken, but I'll keep off it as best I can. Let's . . . get . . . out of here.'

Garner helped Adderly to his feet, and they staggered across the road. He took the helmet with him.

There was a wide strip of ground between the road and the single-track railway. They found a clump of bushes that would suit their purposes. Within the clump, there was enough room for Adderly to recline. Garner got out his pencil torch and began to check out his pilot.

There didn't seem to be as much blood as he'd feared, but Adderly's right arm seemed a mess above the elbow. Missile splinters had chewed through it, although there appeared to be no arterial bleeding. At least that was something.

He ran the torch over the whole of Adderly's body, and decided it would be best to leave his boot on. A fracture would need the support and a sprain – if the boot were removed – would cause the foot to swell so much they'd never get it back on again.

Probably landed badly after ejection, Garner decided.

He checked Adderly's eyes. No dilation, and though he was in pain, Adderly was fully alert. The shock had either not hit him as yet, or he was over it.

There was also a slight swelling by Adderly's right temple. He reached into Adderly's survival kit and got out painkilling tablets and gave him two with sips of water from his bottle. He checked the arm once more. The blood seemed to have formed its own seal and he thought it best not to mess around with it. With a bandage from his own kit he bound the arm carefully, then made a sling out of Adderly's bandage to keep the pilot's forearm across his body.

'How do you feel?' Garner asked. He switched

off the torch and waited for his eyes to get reaccustomed to the dark.

'Keep the day job,' Adderly said with a weak chuckle.

'So I'm no doctor.'

'You've done OK. Thanks for getting us out, and for coming back for me.'

'What makes you think I'd leave you out there?'

'Don't . . . don't mind telling you that I used to think if we ever got into this situation you'd sure be glad to see the last of me.'

Garner thought about that before saying, 'I've had the idea from time to time.'

'You hate me that much?'

'I don't hate you, Nathan. I hate what your family did.'

'That's not *me*. I'm Nathan Adderly, twentieth-century version . . . not . . . not the nineteenth . . .'

'It's your heritage. *My* heritage. It's responsible for the shit that's still in our country.'

Adderly felt silent for a long time.

'Hey!' Garner said. 'Nathan!'

'It's OK. I . . . haven't . . . died on you. Seems we're having our little talk earlier than expected . . . and in a very different place. Wonder what your . . . ball-chewing . . . major's doing right now. Wishing you were with her?' The pain was now making Adderly pause frequently.

'I'm wishing we'll get out of this piece of real estate real soon. I have no taste for a prison camp. Whoever shot at us will have called the dogs out. We'd better try to move on to the RV.'

If troops came on the scene, Garner decided, he'd try to evade and if that failed, they had two pistols between them, and plenty of ammo. There was no way he was going to let either of them go into captivity. He could only hope rescue arrived before matters got that desperate. Things were already bad enough.

'A minute . . . or two,' Adderly was saying '. . . and I'll be . . . ready. Just a . . . minute . . . or two.'

The ball-chewing major had stalked around the room twice and was again leaning against the table, watching the colonel.

The colonel was watching the phone.

'What I need,' Shelley Hoag said, 'is a pool.'

Dempsey stared at her. 'A *swimming* pool?'

'I could do with twenty lengths.'

Wondering if he'd heard correctly, Dempsey went back to looking at the phone.

It rang.

Dempsey stared at it for a moment, then grabbed the receiver. 'Dempsey.'

Shelley Hoag eased herself slowly off the table, a big, sleek cat coming to the alert.

Dempsey got the message he didn't want to hear.

'Cactus down,' he heard.

His hand tightened round the phone. Watching closely, Shelley Hoag knew it was bad news.

'Where?' Dempsey asked.

'According to the position of the short signal, just four miles from the RV. They should make it easy.'

'If they're not hurt. If there are no troops on their trail.'

'We'll have to hope not. Are your boys smart enough to head for cover during the day?'

'They're smart enough.'

'It will be daylight by the time we get to the RV. We'll go in tonight.'

'They'll have to wait the *whole day* out there?'

'If we go in at daylight, Colonel, we're sure as hell going to have a major fire-fight. We'll need air cover, the works. We do this the quiet way,

we should get away with it. All they've got to
do is stay put.'

'And evade troops.'

'We can't go in earlier.'

'I guess not, Colonel,' Dempsey said to the senior Marine officer responsible for dispatching
the rescue mission. 'Keep me informed.'

'I'll do that.'

Dempsey put down the phone. The man with
whom he'd been speaking on the secure line
was on the ship aboard which the two assault
helicopters waited.

He looked at Shelley Hoag. 'No need to tell
you what's happened, Major.'

'No, sir. I'm very sorry.'

'So am I, Major. So am I.'

'I've . . . I've got to stop,' Adderly gasped.

'Sure.'

Garner eased him down by the side of the
road. This was the fourth time Adderly had
called a halt. They had been moving for a while,
but had not covered much distance. Adderly
would appear to be moving along nicely, then
would suddenly gasp and plead to stop. Garner
was worried there were other injuries he didn't
know about, which were perhaps being exacerbated by his trying to get the pilot to the RV.

Yet leaving him behind, even to get to the RV and bring help back, was not an option. Four miles still meant eight miles there and back, even if the helicopters were waiting. Adderly on his own would be easy meat for any troops that came along in the meantime.

Garner also felt that as the darkness would begin to give way to daylight in about an hour, it was very likely that the helicopters would wait for night, making hiding out for the day necessary. They had to get closer to the RV. Perhaps the old man that Shelley Hoag had spoken about would be there to help.

'Here,' Garner said. He broke a piece of chocolate from his kit and put it into Adderly's mouth. 'Some energy.'

'Thanks,' Adderly said, chewing.

'Need a drink?'

'OK . . . for now. Let . . . let's do it.'

'Are you sure you're ready?'

'Ready as I'll ever be. Come on. Help me up. Aarrghh *shit!* No. No. Don't stop. I've . . . got to . . . do it.'

Garner helped him up, and they stumbled on.

8

The squad had watched their missile chase its target all over the night sky and had seen its explosion in the distance, beyond the tops of the trees. Then some time later a vivid flash, much brighter, had lit the night once more. It had been a long way from them, well beyond the trees, but they'd had no doubt what had caused it.

They were jubilant. The squad leader spoke urgently into his radio. He received orders to go and find the wreck.

When the sky began to lighten, Garner took Adderly off the road, across the strip of ground, over the railway track and deep into some woods beyond it. He laid Adderly down, then went in search of a good place to hide out for the day.

After what had seemed ages of looking, he

found something that would do. It was a small cave in a steep, well-wooded section of rising ground. It was still gloomy in the trees, and the cave entrance was heavily screened by thick undergrowth.

He remembered an incident from his childhood when his grandfather had taken him hunting in Georgia.

'Lie on your belly,' Grandpa Garner had said, 'and look along the ground. What do you see?'

It had taken his eyes a long time to focus on what he'd been looking at. It had been a small burrow.

'See it?'

'Yes, Gran'pa.'

'The game's in there, boy. Now let's flush him out.'

Garner had employed the same trick when looking for the cave, and after the third try the thin beam from his pencil torch at last seemed to hit nothing but empty space, between two intertwined, and corded stems in the foliage. He'd struggled his way through, and had found it.

Wondering about wild animals and snakes, he used his torch to cautiously check it out. There was neither, and the place was dry. It looked as if nothing had been in there for years. Perhaps the almost solid screen of undergrowth had made home-hunting animals pass it by. Perhaps it just wasn't suitable. Whatever the reasons for its current vacancy, it was a welcome sight for humans on the run.

He made his way back to where he'd left Adderly. The pilot was lying very still.

'Nathan!' he whispered.

'Don't bust your breeches,' Adderly responded in a surprisingly strong voice. 'Conserving energy.'

'You had me worried.'

'For a man who hates my guts . . .'

'I told you. I don't hate *you* . . . although I still think you shouldn't have waited for me to find out all those things. You could have told me. We were supposed to be friends. Come on. I've found us a place to hide.'

'OK. I'm . . . I'm ready.'

'Getting in there might hurt a little. The bush is almost solid, so we've got to work our way in; but it's a good screen.'

'Like I said . . . I'm ready.'

Garner reached down for him.

'Christ!' Adderly said in horror, leaning heavily against his back-seater. 'I'm . . . I'm never going to get through that!'

The effort to work their way through the

wood to get to the hide had been so great, and had taken so long – despite the short distance involved – that the light was appreciably stronger, and Adderly could clearly see the obstruction.

'You've got to,' Garner told him. 'It's our best chance. The cave is about twelve feet behind that . . .'

'Je . . . Jesus! I'll never make it.'

'You must,' Garner insisted. '*I* can't see it from here, and I know it is there. It's covered from all sides. What better place to hide? It's dry, and there are no animals.'

'But how . . . do I get in?'

'The same way I did. I'll lift some of those bushes to make a sort of tunnel for you while you crawl through on your good elbow and shoulder. I'll go in before you to make the hole. The screen will drop on you as you move in, so try and keep your bad ankle away from it, if you can. When you're in, I'll go back out and make sure we've left no signs for anyone to read out there.'

Adderly stared at the tightly packed foliage. 'I feel like we need one . . . of those . . . machetes you see . . . in all jungle films.'

'No knives. We cut nothing, we break nothing.'

'OK. OK. Let's do it.'

It took some time. Adderly's progress was painfully slow, but he did not complain. At last he got into the cave. There was plenty of room for him to stretch out along its length, with plenty of space between his feet and the entrance. There was also enough room for one other person to lie the same way. Additionally, in the space between him and the entrance, there was sitting room for one, well inside the mouth of the cave. It was still very dark within.

'Hell, you're . . . right,' Adderly said. 'Can't even see . . . daylight from here.'

'It's still a sort of twilight out. We'll be able to see what it's like when the sun's really up. Good thing this isn't one of those wet and wintry Korean days. They would have been able to follow our footprints all the way from that lake. Something to eat? A drink?'

'I'm OK. Just resting . . . after that little . . . workout.'

'All right. I'm going back out to check our trail. I won't be long. You going to be OK?'

'Yes . . . yes.'

'Fine. Just hang in there.'

Garner went back out, spent some time retracing their steps from the time they'd left the railway track. He lay on his stomach behind a screen of low bushes and studied the area for about five minutes. The light was very much brighter now and he could see beyond the track and the road, to the lake. Nothing moved on either the road or the railway. There were no boats on the lake. He could hear no man-made sounds. It was as if there was no one else on the entire planet. A high cloud base of cirrocumulus promised a fine day to come.

He looked at his watch. It was 05.45. They had perhaps gone just one mile since ejecting; a mile – or more realistically, even less – in over two hours. He would have preferred to be closer to the RV. On the other hand, there was probably not such a good location within which to sit out what was going to be a long, fraught day. He wondered where the seats had fallen.

After checking as best he could that they'd left no obvious signs, he worked his way back to the cave. Adderly was dozing

'How're you doing?' Garner asked.

'OK,' Adderly replied drowsily. 'Tired though.'

Garner tested him again for shock, checking the pupils with the torch angled away a little, so that it was not shining in his eyes. He still appeared not to be in shock.

'More chocolate?'

Adderly nodded.

213

Garner gave him another piece, and some water.

'I could . . . use that coffee,' Adderly said.

'You and me both.'

'Is it light . . . out there yet?'

Despite the increasing light outside, none had so far penetrated into the cave.

'It's daylight.'

'None . . . here. Good find, Milt.'

'As the day gets brighter and our eyes adjust, we should be able to see a twilight in here.'

'Something . . . to tell you.'

'I'm listening.'

'You . . . you're an . . . Adderly. Well . . . sort of.'

Garner was sitting with his back against the curve of the cave. He went perfectly still.

'Say what?'

'You . . . are . . . an Adderly.'

His pilot was getting delirious, Garner concluded. There must be other, more serious injuries, probably internal . . .

'You're . . . thinking, his mind's gone . . . ballistic. Am I . . . right?'

'If not,' Garner began carefully, 'what kind of sick game are you playing with me?'

'No . . . game. What you found out . . .

about Nathan Adderly . . . and his daughter's baby . . .'

'You *know* about that?'

'Sure . . . my father . . . gave that journal . . . away. There was . . . is another journal . . . at home. My home. Wait. Let . . . me finish. That baby . . . didn't die. Josiah Adderly, as a boy . . . helped fool . . . his father. With the . . . help of household . . . slave women, he . . . put a . . . dead slave baby . . . in its place. His father . . . never bothered . . . to check. He just . . . wanted it out . . . out of the way. A black baby . . . was a black baby.

'The boy . . . grew up on the . . . plantation. His light . . . skin was passed off as his . . . being the son . . . of one of . . . the white overseers and . . . and a slave woman. It . . . worked . . . because this . . . particular overseer . . . used . . . used to rape . . . her often . . .'

'Jesus. And you wonder why blacks feel the way they do?'

'Are . . . you going . . . to listen . . . or what? You've waited . . . a long time . . . to hear . . . and I . . . to tell.'

'Go on. I'm listening. I'm going nowhere.'

'The boy was . . . called John,' Adderly continued. 'He and Josiah were . . . secret friends until . . . Nathan was killed. Then they became

open . . . friends and . . . of course, Josiah was
also . . . John's uncle. John was not . . . involved
in . . . the killing.'

'What surname did John have?'

'The . . . the . . . overseer's. Unusual name.
Melthorp.'

Garner fell into a stunned silence.

'But that's my . . .' he began at last.

But Adderly interrupted him. 'Your mother's
family . . . name. All over . . . the States . . .
things like that happen. Bound to . . . given
our . . . history. John's father never . . . raped
Helena . . . you know. She . . . loved him. As I've
said . . . you're an Adderly. You're descended
from . . . Helena . . . cousin.'

Adderly gave a weak sigh, and was silent.

'Nathan!'

'Don't shout! I'm . . . OK. Just tired . . .
with all that . . . talking. Good to have
got this . . . off my mind . . . at last. We
named our baby . . . John Milton Adderly.
No more . . . Nathans. Now I want . . . some
rest. OK?'

'Yeah,' Garner said vaguely. 'Sure.'

He was going through an emotional over-
load. Thoughts tumbled one after another as
he tried to come to terms with what Adderly
had said.

Did the pilot's words owe anything to reality? Or was he in the grip of a delirium brought on by his injuries?

But it had sounded like a confession of sorts. And Adderly had called him *cousin*, and had meant it.

In Arizona the previous evening Mason Lyle had been feeling very pleased with himself. It was really neat of the captain to have given him permission to drive the Mustang. He enjoyed working on it, and appreciated being given the opportunity.

What a car! The sound of that engine was totally fantastic. It was the first time he had taken it out since the captain had gone, and he'd wanted to enjoy it all by himself. He had promised the captain he'd look after it even better than his own, and that was exactly what he would do. This was not a joy wagon for his buddies, some of whom had wanted to come with him.

The captain was not like some officers he knew; officers who thought you could gain respect by pulling rank all the time. Captain Garner was different. You could respect a guy who treated you like a human being. When the captain came back, he'd suggest it was time to paint the car. The captain had said he liked metallic blue. Lyle thought that was an excellent colour for the Boss.

He floored the accelerator, and savoured the roar of the 429 engine as the big exhaust pipes echoed in the Arizona night. Then he glanced at the fuel gauge.

'Uh oh. Better put some gas in that tank before I get back to base.'

The base was just thirty miles away, but it was a measure of Mason Lyle's desire to do things the right way that he was reluctant to return the car with less fuel than he'd found in it.

Five miles later he pulled into a service station, just off the minor road he'd been using. There was also a diner, so he decided he might as well grab a bite.

He filled the tank then parked, and went in to eat.

Yannock's pick-up truck pulled in at the station about five minutes later. Amos Brant and Billy Newberg were with him.

Brant jerked upright like a gundog. 'Ain't that the nigger Mustang?'

'Where?' Yannock asked, peering through the windscreen.

'Been at your pecker again? You that blind? Shit, it's over there. By that little yellow, or some faggot colour, foreign sedan. See it?'

'You can't be sure . . .' Yannock began uncertainly.

'Sure I'm sure! Billy! You go look.'

'Amos . . . I don't think . . .'

'Goddamit, Billy! You your daddy's boy, or what? Or maybe a nancy . . .'

'Amos,' Billy said, 'leave it!'

Brant twisted round to glare at Billy. '*Leave* it? *Leave it?* That nigger cost me my licence, boy! I can't drive my truck. You hear me? I can't drive my truck, I got no business. Nobody takes my business from me. I got no fucking licence! Because of that nigger, your pappy took it away!'

It never occurred to Brant to consider that it had all been his own fault.

'I'm not with you on this, Amos . . .'

'Not with me? You scared of your pappy the sheriff? We ain't in your daddy's jurisdiction, Billy. Now go on out and check that car.'

Billy stayed where he was in the back seat while Brant remained twisted round, and continued to glare at him.

The station attendant was looking at them. 'You after some gas? Or you're staying there all night?'

'Smart-ass!' Brant snarled, turning his glare on the attendant.

'Hey! All I asked was if you wanted gas.'

Yannock said, 'Yeah. We want gas. Fill her up.'

'That's all I want to hear.'

Brant poked his head out of the cab. 'You serve that Boss Mustang over there?'

'Nope.'

'Then who?' Brant demanded in exasperation.

The attendant paused. 'What's this? Twenty questions?' He resumed what he was doing.

'Smart-ass!' Brant growled once more, then got out and walked over to where the Mustang was parked.

He made a close inspection of it.

'What's biting your buddy?' the attendant asked.

Both Yannock and Billy were watching Brant.

'Aw . . . he thinks that car belongs to a friend,' Billy replied eventually.

'Sure doesn't act like it,' the attendant said as he completed the fill-up.

He put the hose away, and Yannock got out

to go over to the cashier. When Yannock got back, Brant was standing by the pick-up. The attendant was nowhere to be seen.

'It's the damn car,' Brant said tightly. He glanced up at the sky. 'Good night for a hunt.'

'Amos . . .' Billy began.

'Shut up, Billy! Shut the fuck up! Yannock, you with me?'

Yannock hesitated.

'*You with me, Yannock?*'

After a moment's hesitation, Yannock said, 'I'm with you.'

He got back in behind the wheel, reached behind him, and patted the shotgun clamped in its rack.

Brant gave a nasty smile. 'Good. Now I'm going in there to see if he's eating. You watch to see if he gets into the car.' Brant looked at Billy. 'I don't want to hear it.'

He turned away and walked belligerently towards the diner entrance. They watched him go in.

'I don't like this,' Billy said. 'My father said the guy's an air force officer . . .'

'Out here, in the night, he's just another nigger to me.' Yannock started the pick-up and drove to park in shadow, from where they could keep an eye on the Mustang.

'You guys are crazy. This is gonna go bad . . .'

'Here's Amos.'

Brant was returning. He paused to look around until he saw the pick-up. He didn't look pleased as he approached.

'No niggers in there,' he said as he came up. 'Must be in the john.' He spat. 'Goddam niggers using the same john as white folk. Time we had us a white homeland in this country.'

'How much of it?' Yannock asked.

'*All* of it!' Brant snapped. 'Get rid of anyone who ain't white, and Aryan.'

'What about the Indians, Amos?' Billy Newberg put in. 'They were here long before . . .'

Brant stopped him with a glare. 'You trying to be funny?'

'I just thought . . .'

'Don't think, peckerhead!'

Then the sounds of movement by the diner entrance made them stop to look. People were coming out. None of them was black.

Brant turned to the pick-up once more. 'Must be trying to empty that big black dong of his.'

They all laughed at the coarse joke, Billy

doing so reluctantly. For brief moments, their attention was focused on each other.

The sudden and powerful roar of the Mustang startled them into staring in its direction.

'*Goddamit!*' Amos Brant shouted. 'He must have seen us and waited for a chance to get away!' He hauled himself into the cab. '*Get going, Yannock!* You want him to get away?'

By the time Yannock had got the pick-up moving, the Mustang was on the road and accelerating away.

'We've lost him,' Yannock said. 'That thing's too fast. He beat us last time, and this pick-up is not as fast as yours.'

But Brant was not about to give up. 'We're not beat yet. I know this place. There's a short cut. We can head him off.'

Yannock glanced at him. 'You want me to take *my* pick-up off the road out here, *at night*?'

'I told you I know this place, didn't I? I'll give you directions. Now get this heap moving, goddamit, or we'll lose him for sure. C'mon, c'*mon, Yannock!*'

'What did I tell you?' Brant was triumphant.

They were waiting just beyond a bend, off the road, lights out, ahead of the Mustang.

Yannock and Brant were outside, shotguns in their hands. Billy remained inside.

Then they saw the lights.

'Here he comes,' Brant said softly, as if the driver of the Mustang could hear.

Then the lusty roar reached them.

'Enjoy your last ride, nigger.' Brant raised his shotgun.

Yannock did the same with his own weapon.

Mason Lyle saw the two men in the glare of the headlights and had barely time to register the pump-action shotguns in their hands before the windscreen shattered. There were several rapid explosions, and a terrible pain followed.

Then the world began to tumble.

'*We got him!*' Brant crowed as the Mustang careered off the road.

The spinning car tipped on to its side, then rolled completely three times, its headlights describing crazy arcs as it went. Then the gyrations stopped as it again finished on its side, the headlights pointing accusingly towards the pick-up. It did not catch fire.

Through the pick-up's windscreen, Billy's face looked whitely out on the horrific scene.

'Better finish him off,' Brant said. 'Billy! Give me the flashlight.' He took a couple of paces back and reached with one hand towards Billy Newberg.

Billy did nothing.

'*Get me the goddam flashlight!*' Brant yelled.

Billy jerked out of his stupor and mechanically pulled the powerful torch from its clip, and passed it over.

'Thank *you*!' Brant said with biting sarcasm as he took it. He began walking towards the wreck.

'Watch yourself there, Amos,' Yannock warned. 'Damn-fool thing might explode!'

Brant ignored the advice and was now trotting over to the stricken Mustang, shotgun held ready in one hand, and braced beneath his arm. The twin beams of light from the car seemed to flutter briefly, as he walked through them.

The upper flank of the Mustang was the driver's side, and Brant now slowed as he approached it. He raised the torch, holding it away from his body as he walked cautiously across the remaining distance. He stopped, peered in.

'Oh shit,' he said.

*　　*　　*

'What do you mean: he's *white*?' Yannock asked fearfully, his agitation raising his voice and turning it into a muted squeal.

Blow away a black and mostly, a white jury would not convict. But this was very different. Yannock did not like what the future promised at all.

'*What do you mean: he's white?*' he repeated, panic in his voice now. 'You said . . .'

'I *know* what I said!' Amos Brant cut in sharply 'He *is* white. Can't change that. Maybe that nigger spotted us and got this guy to switch . . . Come see for yourself.'

'I knew this was not good . . .' Billy Newberg began.

'Shut . . . your . . . *mouth*, Billy! You hear? And don't you go telling me you told me so! We're all in this together. Come see for yourself, Yannock. C'mon.'

The fearful, reluctant Yannock went over to the Mustang.

'Oh my God!' he said when he saw Mason Lyle's shattered face. 'Oh my God! Amos, this is big, big shit. Boy! Are we in it! And who the hell is he?'

'How in hell should I know?' was Brant's savage response. 'We'll burn it.'

'*What?*'

'Your ears gone too? We'll burn it! He had an accident.'

'Jesus, Amos! What good will that do? They'll still find all those buckshot holes . . .'

'Get out of the way! I'm gonna torch the tank.' Brant had moved back from the car and was pointing his gun at the rear of the car. 'Get the hell out of there, Yannock!'

Yannock scurried out of harm's way, then stopped to watch apprehensively.

The single shotgun blast made him jump.

Yannock watched with a mind made blank by the fear of the probable repercussions, as Garner's many years of hard work on his pride and joy went up in flames.

And Mason Lyle with it.

'That's strange,' Garner said.

'What's strange?' Adderly enquired in a low voice from within the gloom of the cave.

'I just thought of the Mustang.'

A weak chuckle followed this. 'What do . . . you . . . miss most? The car? Or . . . or the . . . sexy, ball-grabbing major?'

'She hasn't grabbed my balls.'

'Yet. I hear . . . a yet in there some . . . somewhere. And . . . anticipation.'

'You hear too much.'

Another weak chuckle, ending in a single, low cough.

'You all right?' Garner asked anxiously.

'Yes, yes. It's just a . . . slight cough. To a cigarette smoker . . . this would be just . . . a tickle.'

'You don't smoke.'

'Quit it, mother hen.' There was not a second cough.

Garner looked out at the screen of bushes. It was so thick that even though it was now a bright day outside, within the cave a deep twilight remained. Anyone passing would be doing so more than twelve feet away; and as the cave entrance was at foot level before belling out into the chamber itself, he was certain that even someone that close would not realize it was there.

They would be safe until nightfall, when it would be time to try for the RV. He looked across to where Adderly was lying. There was enough difference between the light levels to enable his gloom-adjusted vision to make out his companion quite clearly. He had recently checked Adderly's arm, which had showed no extra sign of bleeding. The ankle was no doubt painful, but the pilot continued to make no complaint.

He had also given Adderly a tablet ration. Garner had decided to conserve the foodstuffs they each carried in their survival vests, in case they had to remain in hiding longer than anticipated. The area would be too hot because of certain pursuit to allow foraging or fishing and still enable them to evade discovery.

Though not strictly a food item, just the one tablet possessed high nutritive value. In addition to relieving thirst and reducing hunger, it produced energy by metabolizing body fat. One of the concentrated tablets – even if that was all that was available – delivered sufficient energy for a man for an entire day. The tablet rations were of particularly immense value if ejection was over the sea.

Garner was glad he had chanced upon the cave. Had he not done so, Adderly would have found the going extremely difficult, perhaps ensuring their eventual discovery by the troops who were undoubtedly searching for them. He again toyed with the idea of leaving his wounded colleague while he struck out for the RV. It was safe enough in the cave.

But again he was reluctant to do so. What if Adderly coughed loudly, just as someone was passing? The cave would act like an echo chamber, and discovery would be inevitable.

Worse, it was virtually certain that jumpy and eager soldiers would simply empty their weapons into the foliage, shredding it, and eventually filling the cave with a barrage of lead and explosives.

I won't leave him, Garner thought.

But there had been times when he'd asked himself what he would have done in such circumstances. He had run the whole gamut: from their current situation, to simply walking out on the man whose family had so brutalized his ancestors. Adderly had been closer to the truth than even he had thought.

But Garner's powerful sense of discipline and responsibility had not let him. He would not have left his pilot to the brutal fate that would certainly be waiting, even if he had not been made aware of the missing section of the astonishing secret history of the Adderly family.

And besides, Arlene would never have forgiven him. *He* would never have forgiven himself.

Garner frowned. But why had he so suddenly thought of the Mustang?

9

'Take . . . a woman . . . like Arlene.'

Adderly had begun to speak so suddenly that Garner, momentarily taken unawares, gave an involuntary start.

'Take . . . someone like . . . Arlene,' Adderly repeated. 'I know . . . I know that some . . . people think . . . she's just a . . . Southern bimbo . . .'

'Nobody thinks that, Nathan.'

'Oh yes . . . some . . . do. Some do. I . . . heard a visiting . . . Falcon jock . . . back at our home . . . base . . . who didn't know shit . . . about her, who'd been . . . looking at her . . . and . . . who didn't realize . . . I was close . . . by. He . . . went on about . . . her . . . her tits and . . . her ass . . . that she was . . . sex on legs . . . but nothing much . . . on top.'

'Take it easy, Nathan. You don't have to

think about this. So some guy was flapping his big mouth . . .'

'Listen! I'm trying . . . to tell you . . . something.'

The sudden intensity in Adderly's voice alarmed Garner. He moved over to where the pilot was lying.

'Nate! You OK, buddy?'

'Sure . . . I'm OK. *Listen* . . . will you?'

'OK, OK. I'm all ears.'

Must be mild delirium, Garner decided. If Adderly wanted to talk about Arlene, let him. It probably helped him to cope with the situation.

'She's . . . she's not . . . like that . . . at all,' Adderly continued. 'Sure, she's got . . . a real . . . nice ass and legs . . . that even . . . Major Hoag would . . . kill for. Hey . . . I married . . . the gal. I know . . . a good thing . . . when I see it. But . . . there's so much . . . more to her. You know . . . what she was . . . like before . . . before we . . . lost the . . . the . . . the baby. You . . . remember?'

'I remember,' Garner said quietly. 'You told me once she looked like a million dollars, and made a man *feel* like a million dollars.'

'Yeah. I . . . remember . . . that.' Adderly gave his weak chuckle, followed by another of the slight coughs. As if knowing what was going on

in Garner's mind, he added, 'Don't ask . . . if I'm
. . . OK. I . . . am, all things . . . considered.'

There was a slight pause, then Adderly
continued. 'Remember . . . something else . . .
I said?'

Garner nodded in the gloom. 'You said I
needed someone like Arlene.'

'Yeah. I did . . . didn't I? Now . . . you take
Major Hoag. Everybody looks . . . at her and
they . . . think . . . razor. There's . . . a woman
. . . with razors for . . . brains, she's so . . . sharp.
She's got . . . that . . . in-your-face . . . don't-fuck
. . . with-me-unless . . . I-say-so look. But I'll . . .
tell you, Milt . . . Arlene's got real . . . guts.
Good, good . . . woman. And . . . she'll still
look . . . as . . . beautiful when . . . she's gone
. . . eighty. The . . . major now . . . the major
. . . will look . . . kind of hard. A man . . . *needs*
. . . a woman like . . . Arlene.'

'What are you saying to me there, Nate?'

'Anything should . . . should happen . . .'

'Nothing's going to happen.'

'*Anything* . . . should happen!' Adderly
insisted, 'you've got . . . to promise me . . .
you'll see that . . . she and young . . . John are
OK. You *must* . . . promise.'

'Will you stop that kind of talk? Nothing's
going to happen. You're going to go home to

your wife and son, if I have to drag you all the way. *They* need *you*. You got that?'

'Promise!' Adderly insisted once more.

'Nathan . . .'

'*Promise!*'

Garner sighed. 'If it means you'll quit this crazy talking, I promise.'

'You'll look . . . after them? Arlene's going . . . to need you . . . there.'

Believing it must be the delirium, Garner decided to humour the pilot. 'I'll look after them.'

'OK.'

'And Nate . . .'

'Yeah?'

'If you go dying on me, I swear I'll beat you to death.'

Adderly chuckled.

It was about 13.00 hours when an airman brought in a single sheet of paper to the colonel.

Dempsey had left the room just once, for a call of nature. Shelley Hoag had also remained. Coffees had been brought to them; but neither had gone to breakfast. Neither seemed keen to go to lunch either.

Dempsey read the message and handed it,

without speaking, to Shelley Hoag, who looked as fresh as if she'd had a full night's sleep.

She read it silently.

'My God,' she then said as she handed it back. 'They've gone public.'

'Good propaganda,' Dempsey commented with dry resignation. '"American imperialists",' he quoted without looking at the sheet of paper, '"invaded our airspace during the night. Our glorious comrades have shot them down and are now hunting out the criminal pilot. He will be found and tried for crimes against the people". How'd I do?'

'Word-perfect.'

'At least they still haven't found the wreckage; or the seats. They said "pilot". One crew member. They don't know it's an Echo Eagle. That's something.'

'They could be lying, to keep us guessing.'

'They could. But whatever the real situation, we don't let them get their hands on those boys.' Dempsey paused. 'We've got to hope that Adderly and Garner are not injured. At least, not seriously enough to cause incapacitation.'

'What if they've already got them?'

Dempsey shook his head. 'They couldn't have stopped themselves from crowing about it. They're holding back on something, but not this. A capture would have been too much to keep quiet about. They need the propaganda, especially with Taiwan shaping up to be the next flashpoint.

'Even if there have been injuries,' the colonel went on, 'they're still mobile, or they've managed to hole up somewhere, to wait till nightfall. As for the three countries involved with the mountain base, they sure as hell won't want too much public light on that little secret. There's going to be some horse-trading, so they badly need to make a capture. They want another TV show, like that time with the helicopter on the southern border. We must make damn sure they don't get it.'

'You know the insertion team's recommendations, sir,' Shelley Hoag reminded him. 'We can't mount the rescue mission till tonight.'

'I know, Major,' Dempsey admitted, curbing his frustration. 'I know. The worst of it is, I have to agree. But if we do . . . *when* we get them out, our friends across the water will suddenly go mighty quiet. They know we've caught them with their pants down. As I've said, there'll be some horse-trading . . . but not with those two boys for bargaining chips. We *must* get them out of there.'

Dempsey rubbed at his nose in quiet agitation. Then as he saw Shelley Hoag watching him, he stopped, looking slightly sheepish.

'Sir,' she began solicitously. 'Why don't you go get some rest? Not much you can do right now but wait.'

'I'm not going down till I know those boys are safe. *They're* not in some cosy bed. What kind of a commander would I be?'

'One who conserves his strength?'

'I'm fine, Major. You go get some sleep.'

She shook her head. 'The colonel stays, I stay.'

Dempsey gave her a tight smile. 'Stubborn too. You worried about Garner?'

'I'm worried about both of them, sir.'

'Now that's a good answer.'

The old man, dressed in the ubiquitous peasant-style jacket and trousers, rode the bicycle slowly along the empty road. There was a covered bamboo basket secured to the pillion. He kept going until he came to the general area where Adderly had landed, then stopped, got off the cycle, and wheeled it to where the pilot had been lying when Garner had found him.

After carefully laying the cycle against a small tree, the old man simply stood there, perfectly still, looking out across the lake. Then he began turning very slowly so that he appeared not to be moving at all, his position altering fluidly.

He studied the ground about him as he turned. When he had finished, he retrieved the bicycle and once more stood for a few seconds, as if waiting for something to happen. His head again turned slowly, his eyes missing nothing.

Then once again he stood still. His gaze was locked upon the high, wooded ground beyond the railway track. He seemed convinced of something.

He mounted the bicycle, and rode back the way he had come.

'You know . . . Helena had the . . . most beautiful . . . grey eyes.'

'Hell, Nathan! Quit startling me like that! I never know when you're going to start talking. I thought you were grabbing some zees.'

The familiar soft chuckle came out of the gloom, and Garner primed himself for the cough to follow, but there wasn't one.

'As I said . . . Helena . . . your ancestor . . . had grey eyes . . . like yours . . . like mine. Arlene noticed that . . . straight off . . . first time she . . . saw you . . . and me . . . together. And here . . . we are in this . . . in a cave . . . in a country . . . far from ours . . . where . . . no one can . . . see our . . . eyes. Crazy life . . . huh?'

Then the cough arrived. It was more pro-
longed than any of the previous ones and when
it was over, Adderly sounded short of breath.

Garner switched on his torch to look at
him.

'Hey!' Adderly said. 'Trying . . . to blind . . .
me? Put . . . the darned thing . . . out.'

'Just checking you out.'

'I'm OK. Just . . . a cough.'

Garner put out the torch. He had checked
round Adderly's mouth, but could see nothing
amiss. He went back to his sitting position by
the mouth of the cave.

Long before, he'd removed his G-suit, and
had folded it so as to make a pillow for Adderly's
head to rest upon. The pilot had now moved off
it, during the bout of coughing, so Garner slid
it gently back beneath his head.

'Want something to drink – or eat?' he
asked.

'No . . . thanks. Not hungry. Not thirsty. Did
I tell you . . . about Arlene?'

'You told me.'

'Hell of . . . a woman. I ever . . . told you
. . . she once knocked . . . a guy flat on . . .
his ass?'

'Haven't heard that one. When did this
happen?'

Better to let him continue to talk about Arlene, Garner decided. It was obvious that thinking about her kept him in good spirits.

'I think we . . . were in some . . . shopping mall . . . somewhere,' Adderly said. 'Can't . . . can't quite . . . remember. I'd left . . . her by a perfume counter . . . and this . . . jerk came up . . . to her and put . . . his hand on . . . her ass. She was . . . wearing . . . short shorts.' A soft chuckle as he remembered. 'Boy! She zapped that . . . guy right in . . . the kisser. I mean . . . *zap*!'

'What did she use?'

'Use? Her *fist*! She's got . . . a mean right . . . hand. Remember that. The guy went . . . down. I don't mean . . . staggered. He went . . . *down*. Right on his . . . ass. I was . . . proud of . . . her. That's my . . . Arlene.'

Adderly was suddenly quiet, as if the talking had exhausted him. Garner, again anxious, began to move back to check on him. But Adderly sensed the movement.

'You're . . . fussing again, Milt. Sit down. I'm just . . . having another rest.'

'OK.'

Arlene had woken suddenly without quite knowing why.

A weak night light was on, near the baby's cot. She looked anxiously at the infant, wondering if perhaps he had whimpered in his sleep, triggering her mothering instincts. Her highly alert state was another legacy of the loss of the first baby.

But he was peacefully sleeping the night away, as always.

She glanced at the digital alarm clock. It was 1.30. So why had she woken, if not for the baby?

She sat up in bed, pondering upon it for some moments, trying not to think it was anything to do with Nathan. She always worried about him.

But what wife of the fighter crews didn't?

Every wife and girlfriend she'd spoken to about it when she had first got married had told her essentially the same thing in her own way. Each coped according to her own personality. Some looked upon it as part of the territory, and had long come to terms with the fact that they knew what they had been getting into, before they'd done the deed. There was little point in making a big deal about it. But one thing Arlene was certain of: they all worried.

There was a small television set on a bedside table, with headphones attached. She propped herself up against the pillows, turned on the set, and put on the headphones. She switched on the TV. It came on in the middle of a newsflash.

'. . . and they claim . . .' the anchorman was saying, 'to have shot down a Western military aircraft, in the early hours of the morning, local time. There is as yet no confirmation. I'll repeat that: *no* confirmation. We'll bring you more news about this incident directly. But now, to Joanne Marr in Washington for a Pentagon comment, and Don Yamuchi in Tokyo . . .'

Arlene raised her hand to her mouth slowly. 'Oh no,' she whispered, dreading to hear more. 'Please don't let it be Nate and Milton. Please, God. Not them.'

When they went on their various deployments, Nathan did not always call if, for operational reasons, it was not feasible to do so. As far as she knew, he was still out there in Arizona. So why should she worry if something had happened way out in the Far East?

She could always call to check with the base. But she was reluctant to do anything that might reflect badly on Nathan.

She turned off the TV, as if suddenly repelled by it. Removing the headphones, she placed them with exaggerated care on top of the set, before folding her arms tightly across her chest.

She remained propped up against the pillows, staring at the baby's cot, hugging herself, and shaking.

At the mountain base, Major Udlov strode towards the room where he was to be interviewed by the three commanders of the unit.

Colonel Peng was Senior Officer Commanding. Colonel Krashinev was First Deputy Commander and Colonel Ongg, North Korean, Second Deputy Commander. All were experienced fighter pilots. Though officially of equal status, everyone, especially the Russian aircrew and ground personnel, knew this was a face-saving exercise. In reality, Krashinev was the true commander. Russian personnel irreverently called them the Troika. Udlov was well aware of this, having heard the term used by some of his own fellow officers.

Udlov had been picked up by helicopter within forty-five minutes of being shot down. Unlike Garner and Adderly, he'd had the luxury of being able to keep his location beacon continuously transmitting, without fear of being captured.

But Udlov was not feeling particularly happy. He had already been grilled by the unit's three intelligence officers – another troika, he mused sourly – and the general consensus was that he should not have allowed himself to be shot down.

You should have been there, he'd thought grimly, listening to their waffle. How well would you have done?

None of the intelligence officers – one of whom was a woman and the North Korean representative – had any flying experience. It had galled him to listen to them questioning tactics they clearly knew very little about.

He enjoyed the reputation of being the ace of the base. He was also the senior fighter instructor. But the fact that he had not only lost his best pupil among the Koreans, but had himself been vanquished by the as-yet-unknown Westerner, was doing that reputation no good at all. Last night's events, he knew, would seriously dent it. He would have to do some rapid retrieval, and he believed he knew how best to accomplish that. It helped to know that Ling had made it back.

He would be pleased when the Western pilot, if still alive, was eventually caught. He would like to meet the man who had cost him two Su-27Ks, a promising student, *and* dealt his reputation such a blow, face to face. There was one way to ensure it.

Udlov was in a foul temper. The only thing that alleviated this was the fact that the other pilot had not yet escaped, and was even now endeavouring to avoid capture; if he had survived the hit by the surface-to-air missile.

Ready for anything, Udlov marched into the room and saluted smartly.

'We will not stand on ceremony, Comrade,' Colonel Peng began immediately, speaking Russian. 'Please sit down.'

Udlov knew that Peng's rapid opening of the proceedings had less to do with putting him at ease than with establishing the pecking order over his fellow colonels. As representative of the base's host country, he clearly felt this was the correct state of affairs.

'Thank you, Comrade Colonel,' Udlov said respectfully and sat down on the straight-backed chair that had been placed there for him.

'We have the intelligence report on your combat,' Peng continued, clearly intent on keeping the initiative over the others. 'Now we would like to hear of it from you.'

Udlov glanced at Krashinev, who gave him the barest perceptible sanction. Peng caught the glance and for the most fleeting of seconds, he looked annoyed.

Then Udlov gave a factual account of what

had occurred, making no embellishments. When he had finished, it was the Korean who looked offended.

'Are you blaming Captain Yeung for this . . . fiasco?' he demanded.

Fiasco, Udlov thought contemptuously.

There was another North Korean senior officer, a lieutenant colonel, who sometimes deputized for Ongg. Udlov had a lot of time for him. The lieutenant colonel would have understood the situation, without waving national dignity in everybody's face. Udlov frequently thought the appointments were in the wrong order. Ongg should have been the underling.

'With great respect, Comrade Colonel,' he now said, 'I strongly advised him against precipitate action. As both my student and my wingman, he was under my orders.'

'Captain Yeung cannot speak for himself.'

'He brought about his own death.' Udlov was unrepentant.

The North Korean colonel bristled, but Udlov steamrollered through the possible interruption.

'When you have listened to the cockpit recordings, sir,' Udlov continued, 'you'll hear me clearly forbidding him to attack while he was still out of position. He was to follow my lead. I believe he wanted to make a kill over the border, for glory.'

'*How dare you!*' Ongg snapped. 'You are besmirching a noble comrade!'

Udlov was still irritated by the interview with the intelligence officers, and was in no mood to be lectured by anyone, particularly Ongg. He was the best Su-27K pilot around and if they wanted to relieve him of his command, that was their affair. The entire training programme would grind to a halt, as the other instructors would not be happy with the change.

'I *dare*, Comrade Colonel,' he now said, 'because I have spent several weeks pounding the correct procedures into the dead noble comrade's head! It was his *first* night flight, and the first time he was carrying live weapons. No one expected to find a hostile fighter right on our doorstep. Ground control didn't warn us until too late! In such circumstances, it was insane of him not to have listened to someone of experience; to have ignored his superior officer and senior instructor! Perhaps he even panicked. I *won't* accept the blame for someone who disobeys orders, and is then killed by his own folly! Compare *that* with Captain Ling, who brought back his severely damaged aircraft.'

Udlov stopped, eyes unflinchingly holding on to the Korean colonel's. It was Peng who stepped in to cool things down.

'Yet you, an experienced fighter pilot, were shot down.' The Chinese colonel spoke softly, clearly impressed by Ling.

'I make no excuses,' Udlov said. 'He surprised me, and he was good.' He knew his comments about Ling had gone down well.

'You sound as if you admire the intruder.'

'If an opponent is good, there is no disgrace in honouring him, even if you want his destruction.'

Peng inclined his head slightly. 'A commendable attitude which finds favour with me. Nevertheless, this foreigner has done us considerable damage and cannot be allowed to get away with it. If he is still alive, he must be found before the imperialists attempt to rescue him.'

'If I may be permitted,' Udlov said, 'I would like to lead the hunt. During the recent rapprochement with the West, I had the opportunity to visit some of their units and talk with their pilots. I believe I have a general idea of how they would behave under these circumstances. I may know what to look for. I also want the squad who fired the missile that brought down the foreigner to be placed under my command.'

Peng looked at Krashinev, who had not spoken at all but had been observing the entire proceedings keenly. The Russian's eyes now held his compatriot's gaze.

Still looking at Udlov, Krashinev gave another of his barely perceptible signals.

'I think it's a good idea,' he remarked.

The North Korean colonel looked outraged, but chose not to raise any objection.

The old man did not look up when he heard the helicopter. He was sitting at the edge of the lake, his bicycle lying on its side next to him. The woven bamboo basket was close to hand.

The helicopter, a huge predatory insect bearing the insignia of the three allied countries, touched down a hundred yards away.

A squad of soldiers leapt out.

The helicopter rose into the air once more, almost before the last man hit the ground. The aircraft, a Mil Mi-24 assault gunship, originally dubbed the Hind by NATO, was heavily armed and armoured. This was an advanced version with a full complement of radar and infrared sensors, and carried four rocket pods beneath its mid-mounted stub wings. It also had fixed twin 23mm guns mounted on the right side of its nose. Wheeling about within its own length, it headed off the way it had come.

The soldiers approached the old man at a fast trot. When they had come to within a few yards, they stopped and fanned out. The junior NCO leading them strode arrogantly towards him. They were the same North Korean squad who had shot down Adderly and Garner.

'*You!* Old man! What are you doing here?'

'Fishing,' the old man replied calmly, 'as you can see. I have been fishing here for years. And have you no respect for your elders?' He reached into his peasant's jacket and took out a small document. 'I am permitted.'

'And have you caught anything?'

'Alas . . . so far today, the fish are smarter than I am.' The old man gave a deprecating shrug.

'What's in that basket?'

'Food. You may look if you wish.'

'I do not need your permission!'

The squad leader stared at the old man coldly, but made no move to check the basket. At last, he deigned to look at the document.

While he was doing so the soldier who had fired the missile stared quizzically at the old man.

The squad leader handed back the document,

and was slightly less belligerent. 'Have you seen anyone else around here?'

'Should I have?'

'Just answer me!'

'But what kind of person?'

'That is none of your affair!'

'Then how am I to know if I have seen the right person?'

'I said *anyone*! That is all you need to know!'

'Then I have seen no one. I have been here all alone.'

'Why did you not say so in the beginning?' the squad leader demanded crossly.

'You confused me,' the old man replied apologetically.

'You are very far from your village.'

'I often go long distances on my bicycle,' the old man explained. 'The people of my village know this. I have done this for years also.'

The squad leader made a dismissive sound and went back to his men. The one who had fired the missile spoke urgently to him. The squad leader stiffened, then strode back to the old man.

'One of my men believes he knows you.'

The old man turned to peer at the other soldiers, squinting against the bright sun.

'My eyes . . .' he began. 'They are not as they used to be . . .'

'He says you come from his village, and that you are the father of a comrade, a glorious fighter pilot.'

'I do have a son who flies one of those machines, yes. I don't know how he does it. I would not go into one of these things . . .'

'He is doing good work protecting us against the imperialist dogs. He is protecting you so that you can fish in freedom!'

'I am very proud of him.'

The squad leader had become respectful now. He stood to attention as he spoke. 'You should have told me who you are.'

'One should not boast. We all serve our glorious country in our own way.'

'Yes. Yes. You are correct. We must now be on our way. We are hunting enemies of the people.'

'Then I wish you success.'

'Thank you, respected Comrade.'

The squad leader was now courtesy itself. He saluted the old man and went back to his men. He bawled out orders and the entire group trotted off. They did not go across the railway track, towards the woods.

The old man watched them leave, then

glanced in the direction of the high ground. He looked down at the basket and made no move to take anything to eat from it.

He calmly went back to his fishing.

In the cave, both Garner and Adderly had heard the sound of rotors.

'Ours?' Adderly asked in a sharp whisper.

'Not a chance,' Garner replied. 'They wouldn't be crazy enough to do this in daylight. The hunting dogs have been let loose.' He cocked his automatic pistol as softly as he could, and waited. 'Sounds like it's moving away.'

'Perhaps . . . they've dropped . . . troops.'

'Could be.'

'If that . . . chopper's got . . . heat sensors . . .'

'We're safe in here. Those sensors would have to try to see right through this mountain. And we've been in here long enough not to have left any traces outside.'

'As long as . . . they don't . . . use real . . . dogs.'

'Yeah,' Garner agreed. 'That could give us a problem. But first, they've got to have an idea of where we may be. If they haven't found the airplane, they won't know how many people they're looking for. Hell, pieces of the bird must be all over the place anyway.

It could take them months, maybe years, to find it all.'

'Did I . . . just hear . . . you cock . . . that pistol?'

'You did. They won't take us. Not alive, that's for sure. But we will be getting out of here. I'm going to get you back to Arlene, and to your boy.'

'That's a promise . . . is it?'

'It is. Besides, she'd never forgive me if I didn't.'

'She'd . . . understand . . . if she knew . . . what really happened.'

'She won't have to, because you're going to be right there.'

'Not . . . trying to be . . . a VF-32 . . . hero . . . in reverse, are you?'

'What? VF-32? That's *Navy*.'

Was Adderly going into another bout of delirium? Garner wondered. What was all this about a Navy squadron? And what was happening in reverse?

'The Swordsmen,' Adderly was saying. 'Korea, 1953. They had . . . a black Ensign. First black . . . Navy aviator. He was . . . giving air support . . . to the Marines . . . at Chosin. Hit by . . . ground fire. He crash . . . landed on . . . a rough-as-hell . . . mountain . . . slope. He got down . . . OK . . . but was trapped . . . in cockpit. His white . . . buddy force . . . landed his . . . own plane . . . to try . . . rescue. Tried to . . . put out the fire . . . on his buddy's . . . plane with bare . . . hands. The black . . . guy died in . . . the end. They both . . . got medals. The guy . . . who died . . . got the post . . . posthumous DFC. The other guy . . . got the . . . Medal of Honour . . . from the President . . . too . . .'

Adderly lapsed into silence.

For a while, Garner too was silent as he thought about Adderly's story of the Navy pilots.

'The only medal I want,' he eventually said in a quiet voice, 'is the smile on Arlene's face when she sees you. OK?'

'But what if . . .'

'*OK?*'

'Sure.'

Udlov was in a second Mi-24. As heavily armed and comprehensively equipped as its sister machine, it clattered low over the dense covering of a mountainside. It was thirty-five kilometres from where Garner and Adderly lay hidden, and going away from them.

In the cabin of the helicopter, Udlov was strapped to his seat staring at one infrared, and one radar monitor that had been specially rigged up for him. Everything that the co-pilot gunner in the forward of the two bulbous cockpits saw would be relayed to him. As yet, nothing of interest had appeared on either screen.

In the seven other seats were three Russian and four Chinese soldiers. The crews of both helicopters were also Russian. All were under Udlov's overall command, but with a Russian captain in charge of the combined assault troops.

If the pilot who had shot him down had managed to get out before being hit by the missile, Udlov now reasoned, the ejection seat should be within the area. If the hit had been too quick to allow ejection, then pieces of the aircraft would soon come to light. In the case of the first scenario, he hoped to get to that pilot well before a rescue was mounted.

On the ground, some two kilometres from Garner and Adderly, the squad passed within twenty feet of where Adderly's seat lay, half buried in an abundantly overgrown gully. It had thumped itself down there, even as the Echo Eagle was being consumed by its fuel and the detonated charges.

The squad kept going.

10

'*Arlene!*'

The loudly whispered name had Garner scrabbling over to Adderly's side. 'Nate! You OK?'

'Wh . . . what? Oh. Yeah. Sure. What did . . . I do?'

'You called Arlene. Louder than normal. I kind of wondered if . . .'

'No sweat. I'm . . . I'm OK. Must have . . . dreamed . . . I guess.'

'Here. Let me check you over.'

'No . . . need. I'm fine.'

'I'll do it, anyway. I won't move you. Just a routine inspection.'

'Did I say . . . you were . . . a mother . . . hen?'

'Yeah, yeah. You did.'

'That's not . . . going to . . . stop you . . .'

'Nope.'

A sigh. 'I guess.'

Garner had got out his torch and was looking Adderly over even as they spoke. The arm still did not seem to have bled further. He looked at the booted, damaged ankle. Little point in unlacing it until they had access to proper medical attention.

He checked Adderly's head, but did not touch it. Adderly seemed comfortable enough. However, Garner was worried about the swelling by the temple, which seemed to have grown slightly.

He put out the light.

'Is . . . is it me?' Adderly began. 'Or . . . does this . . . cave seem darker?'

'The day's nearly done. It's just after 17.00 hours. Soon be night, and we can get out of here. They haven't found us, so just hang in there a little longer. Need a drink, or a bite?'

'No. That tablet's . . . still working.'

'All right. Look . . . I'm going to grab me a little shut-eye. But I'll be right here by the entrance. Just sing out if you want anything. I'll just be having a catnap.'

'Go right ahead. You've been . . . awake all this . . . time while I've been getting all . . . the sleep. Go . . . go on. I'll yell . . . if I hurt too . . . much.'

'Not a yell. Please! Think of the neighbours!'

Adderly chuckled. The cough didn't sound. 'See?' he said triumphantly. 'No cough.'

Garner smiled in the gloom and shut his eyes, to try and get some sleep.

It was the Hind that had dropped the Korean squad that made the first discovery.

The co-pilot/gunner, searching with both radar and infrared sensors, caught something motionless on radar. They went closer to investigate. Hovering close to some treetops, they were astonished to discover the Echo Eagle's completely intact tailplane. It was lying on the top branches, twenty-five kilometres from the cave, and its only blemish was a large scorch mark on its upper surface. It was 18.00 hours local time.

They informed Udlov immediately.

The second Mi-24 arrived on the scene within twenty minutes and stood off to one side. Sliding down from their helicopter, two Russian soldiers hung by their ropes from their hovering aircraft, and secured the tailplane in a harness. With the two men and the captive tailplane now dangling beneath it, the helicopter, in company with Udlov's, moved away from the trees to a patch of open ground about a kilometre away.

Udlov's machine touched down, while the soldiers hanging from the other Mi-24 dropped the few feet to the ground. Then the tailplane was put gently down, and the harness released. The Mi-24 then landed.

Udlov hurried to inspect the find. Light was fading in the clearing, and he used a torch to do so.

'This is from an Eagle,' he said. 'See that dog-tooth here at the leading edge? An Eagle,' he repeated.

So that's what he'd been up against. Had the pilot survived? He had a sudden thought. An Eagle. What if it had been the advanced *Eagle E*? There could be *two* crew members. An even bigger coup.

He glanced up at the darkening sky. 'Everybody gather round,' he ordered and when they had done so, went on, 'The light's going, but that does not matter. We're going to work all night, and all day tomorrow and beyond, if necessary. We'll give our search area a radius of thirty kilometres from this point. Look for the ejection seat. There may also be two crew members, so you may find two seats. Look for more bits of the aircraft, parachutes, helmets, discarded flight clothing . . . anything that points to the downed American.'

He stopped and got out a map of the area from his flight overalls, then walked over to the port stub wing of the nearest helicopter and laid the map on it.

They followed, forming a loose group about him.

He drew a rough circle, using their current position as its centre. He then quartered the circle and numbered each segment clockwise.

He looked at the Russian captain. 'Arkady, you and your men take sector one.'

Arkady Litiniev nodded.

'I'll take sector two,' Udlov continued, 'using the squad that was dropped off by that small lake. We'll pick them up when we leave here, so you can have their chopper. I'll be calling up two more 24s, each with troops, and give them the information for sectors three and four. They can go directly to their assigned area.

'I want you all to look for *anything* and *everything*. As I've said, we may actually have two of them out there, if they survived the SAM. You've got your night-sights. Find him, or them. We want a prisoner, or prisoners. Not dead bodies . . . unless we find them that way. And we want them *before* the Americans come for them.'

'And if we can't do that?' In the gathering gloom, Litiniev's eyes were shadows. 'If we can't take him . . . them alive?'

'*Alive*, Arkady,' Udlov said quietly. 'All right, everybody. Go to it!'

They ran to their machines. Soon, the predator insects were lifting off the ground. From his helicopter, Udlov called up the Korean squad and made a rendezvous.

The cave where Garner and Adderly were hiding fell neatly into sector three.

Garner awoke suddenly. He looked at the glow on his watch: 19.00 hours. He'd been down longer than he'd intended.

'Nathan!'

'I'm here.'

Garner felt a huge relief, and moved over. 'How are you feeling?'

'OK. But my . . . head's . . . slipped off the . . . speed jeans.'

'Soon fix that.'

Garner shone the torch briefly to find the rough pillow, then placed it back beneath Adderly's head.

'Thanks,' the pilot said.

'It's going to be time to be heading to the RV soon, Nate,' Garner said. 'I've thought hard about this and I want you to tell me if you can move. The truth now. I don't want to leave you here in case that chopper comes back. But when we're out there, we could be sitting ducks for night-sights. Our choppers will have a doctor and a medic aboard. It might make better sense for me to go out and bring them back, instead of my doing you more damage by dragging you three or four miles . . .'

'Could you . . . love someone . . . like Arlene?' Adderly posed the question instead of replying to Garner.

'*What?* What are you saying now, Nathan?'

'Could . . . you . . . love someone . . . like Arlene?'

'Any man with red blood . . .'

'Could *you*? I know . . . you . . . understand the . . . question.'

'What is this? You're passing your wife on to me now?'

'I want you . . . to look . . . after her. She's . . . going to need . . . you.'

'Hey, man. You're scaring me. Don't talk like that.'

'Makes . . . makes . . . sense.'

'That kind of talk does *not* make sense! You just hang on in there, Nathan Adderly. You hear me?'

'I . . . hear . . .'

'And before you know it we'll be on that chopper, heading away from this place. Like that.'

Garner clicked the fingers of his right hand. Only there was no clicking sound. The fingers felt sticky. He must have touched a bug and squashed it, he decided, and tentatively sniffed at them in the dark. He expected a pungent smell. What he got made his heart suddenly beat faster.

He shone the torch on the folded G-suit, and felt as if he'd been hit in the stomach. A smear of bright blood was on the fabric. But where from?

Then he saw the corners of Adderly's mouth. Internal bleeding. The worst. Lungs.

Even as he watched, Adderly coughed and the blood welled out of him.

'Jesus, Nate! Why didn't you tell me?'

Heart in mouth, Garner gently removed the G-suit pillow, enabling Adderly to lie flat, then moved the pillow to the legs, to raise them off the floor of the cave. Keeping the legs higher would help the heart pump blood upwards, but short of wiping Adderly's mouth periodically, there was very little else he could do. Adderly needed urgent medical care.

'Tell . . . you . . . what?'

'You're hurt inside . . .'

Garner stopped. Adderly *had* been telling him. All that stuff about Arlene . . .

Adderly sensed Garner's realization. 'Now . . . now you . . . know.'

'I'm getting you out!'

'Move me . . . and you . . . kill me . . . anyway . . .'

Garner was distraught. 'Nate! You can't do this.'

'I . . . didn't . . . the SAM . . . did . . .' Adderly's voice faded.

Garner sat in the dark cave, listening to his friend die and felt the tears in his eyes.

This just isn't right, he thought helplessly.

Adderly had needed urgent medical attention, virtually from the moment he'd landed after ejection. Internal injuries were enemies of time.

What was Nathan Adderly doing so far from home, dying in a cave on a Korean hillside? What of the baby boy he should be watching grow up?

'And what am I going to say to Arlene?' he said aloud.

'Tell . . . her . . . you love . . . her . . .'

'Nathan! You're going to be OK!'

'Shh . . . !'

Garner felt a hand groping for his, and held on to it.

'Gentlemen!'

Garner jerked at the sound of the voice outside the cave, then remained absolutely still. It was then that he realized there was an abnormal heaviness about Adderly's hand.

He felt for a pulse. There was none. When had Adderly died?

'Gentlemen!' came the voice again.

Garner drew his pistol.

'I know you are in there,' the voice said pleasantly. 'No need to cock your weapons. I am a friend.'

Garner said nothing.

'I will give you a short history. Perhaps you will then believe me. In 1951, a pilot was shot down. He did not return to his homeland, but remained here. Is this a help?'

Garner still waited. North Korean Intelligence might easily know that story.

'I will say a name,' the voice continued. 'Green Ringer. Please hurry. The helicopter and the troops will be back. Perhaps with reinforcements. I have been waiting all day to make contact.'

Garner still waited.

'How about Cactus?'

That got Garner's attention.

What the hell, he thought after a while. I can't stay in here for ever.

He began to make his way out of the cave. When he was eventually outside, his gloom-accustomed eyes made out the figure of an old man.

'At last!' the man said. 'You can put away your gun. I am a friend. Where is your colleague? We must hurry. I have brought food. You can eat on the way. This is a very good hiding place that you have found. I once used it myself, a long time ago.'

'He's dead,' Garner said flatly.

'Ah. I am sorry . . .'

'I'm not leaving him in there.'

The old man was silent and Garner knew he was being scrutinized.

'I understand,' the old man said at last. 'I, too, once lost many close friends. I have a bicycle. We shall manage.'

With some difficulty, they finally got Adderly's body out of the cave. The old man had brought more than food in the basket. They used lengths of light rope to tie Adderly to the bike and, supporting it on either side, they walked down the slope and on to the road.

They began walking towards the RV.

*   *   *

The squad had found nothing by the time Udlov's helicopter had picked them up.

As it beat across its designated area of search, the squad leader spoke to Udlov.

'We saw an old man by the lake today, Comrade Major.'

Udlov looked at him. 'Why did you not mention this on the radio?'

'He was fishing. He frequently fishes there. He has papers of authority.'

'What has that got to do with it? He might have seen something, or someone.'

'I interrogated him. He had seen no one. I also discovered . . .' The squad leader paused, clearly uncomfortable.

'Yes?'

The NCO cleared his throat, looked round at his men.

'Are you addressing me? Or them?'

'You, Comrade Major.'

'Then please continue.'

'The old man has a son in the People's Air Force.'

'I see. What is this son's status?'

'He is a lieutenant colonel.'

Udlov stared at the NCO. 'I see,' he repeated. 'And this officer's name?'

The NCO told him.

It was the name of the deputy to Colonel Ongg.

'My son is also a fighter pilot,' the old man was saying conversationally.

'Like you used to be.'

'Yes.'

'Isn't what you're doing against what he stands for?'

'On the contrary. He wants a democratic nation, and does not want this country to be involved in another war. The only way is to eventually merge with the South, democratically. A war would bring suffering far worse than the one which first brought me here. We desire the same thing. He believes that for real change to occur, you must be on the inside. He is a lieutenant colonel at the base.'

Garner nearly lost his grip on the bicycle. '*He* gave you the information?'

'Oh no. He is not involved in this. My squadron was wiped out by your Sabres,' the old man went on. A sad note had crept into his voice. 'It is ironic to meet you, an American airman, here. Our squadron commander, a fierce pilot in combat, was killed. Such a beautiful woman, our Valentina.' He paused, remembering. 'I believe she was in love with one of your pilots.'

Garner remembered the strange story Shelley Hoag had told. It seemed incredible; but in wartime many strange things happened. The old man's own history was a case in point.

'How can you be sure?' he asked.

'They met during the end-of-war celebrations,' the old man said. 'I believe they even kissed.' He sighed. 'Life is sometimes most cruel. In a better world, they might have become man and wife. Who knows? He was the only one who could have beaten her in combat. And he did.'

For a while they walked the bicycle, with its dead rider, in silence.

'You were close?' the old man began once more. 'You and your friend?'

'He is family,' Garner said.

If the old man thought that strange, he made no comment about it.

'It is even harder,' he said, 'when the lost one is family.'

Garner nodded in the darkness and said nothing. He walked on, feeling the weight of Adderly's body against his left shoulder.

The rescue mission was on its way.

The two Blackhawk helicopters skimmed the water, escorted by two Apache gunships spread out on either side, and holding station. They were there to deter any interference with the mission. The Blackhawks' crews were, like the troops they carried, and the doctor and medical assistant, US Marines. The Apaches were also flown by Marines.

Before they'd left, the briefing had been to the point.

'Go in,' their colonel had said. 'Get them, and get out. We're not looking for a fight, but if anyone tries to stop the mission . . . waste him.'

They had cheered loudly. Soon, they would be crossing ultra-low, over the coast.

Udlov's gunship made the next find. They spotted a big chunk of the Echo Eagle lying half-submerged in a fast-flowing stream, some fifteen kilometres north of the cave.

The gunship settled down near a bank and Udlov and his Korean troops climbed out. Using night-vision binoculars, he studied what looked like a long piece of the side of the cockpit.

The squad leader started moving towards the stream.

'Stay where you are!' Udlov ordered in Korean. He kept looking at the piece of the aircraft, then he took the glasses away from his eyes and spoke into the radio attached to his flight suit. 'Turn on your landing lights,' he said to the pilot.

The lights came on, shining clearly on the chunk of aircraft in the water.

'All right,' he said to the NCO. 'Take a man and get it out. Be careful of booby-traps.'

'Yes, Comrade Major.'

The NCO called to one of his men and together, they waded into the stream. They had to struggle to get it out, because it had embedded itself into the bottom of the stream.

Udlov sent a third man to help. Eventually they managed it, and dragged the piece of wreckage to the bank.

Udlov saw the two inverted black triangles with the word 'DANGER' stencilled along each side, and within the triangles the white stencilled captions 'EJECTION SEAT' and 'CANOPY'.

'And now we know,' Udlov remarked softly. 'Two cockpits. An Eagle E. There are *two* of them!' he went on to the troopers. 'We'll note the location and leave this for the salvage teams. Now back on board! Let us find these Americans!'

'Now all we have to do,' the old man said, 'is wait.'

They had arrived at the RV, which was a kilo-metre beyond the road and the southern shore of the lake; it was virtually on the coast.

From where he stood, Garner could make out distant lights, way out to sea. He knew those lights did not belong to the ships from which the rescue was being mounted. They would be well out of harm's way, beyond the horizon.

Then he heard rotors, coming from inland.

'This is not good,' he said. 'You should get away from here,' he went on to the old man. 'If they should find you . . .'

'I shall leave when your people arrive.'

They had untied Adderly, and laid him gently behind a screen of bushes large enough to hide them all.

But for how long?

'I can't ask you to do that,' Garner said.

'You're not asking me. It is my wish. If you listen, you may hear something on the breeze from the sea.'

Garner could hear nothing. 'I have perfect hearing, but . . .' He paused, listening. 'Yes! I hear rotors.'

'I shall leave now. You no longer need me.'

Not knowing what else to do, Garner stuck

out a hand. 'I cannot thank you enough. I am very sorry about your Valentina.'

The old man took the hand and shook it. 'That is the tragedy of our profession. I am sorry about your . . .'

'Cousin,' Garner said.

'Your cousin.'

'I hope your son succeeds.'

'It would be a worthwhile thing.'

Then the old man was leaving as the sound of rotors grew louder. In moments, he seemed to have disappeared.

Garner turned on his beacon briefly.

In the lead Blackhawk, a crewman said, '*Beacon!* They're at the RV!'

'OK, hogs!' the mission commander said into his radio. 'In and out. Fast.'

Then he heard from one of the Apaches. 'We have company! Moving to intercept.'

'Don't fire unless they do!'

'Roger. No engagement unless attacked.'

'Let's hope they feel the same way,' the rescue mission commander said to himself.

The Blackhawks crossed the coast.

'I've got helicopters!' the pilot of the Mi-24 in sector three called to Udlov's helicopter urgently, as he studied his radar. 'Four! Two are moving on an intercept course. Probably Apaches.'

Udlov fully understood what that meant. The Americans would fight to rescue their men. And the Apaches could make life exceedingly difficult. But would they attack first?

'On our way! Get the others to join us as quickly as they can,' he added to his pilot. 'They must *not* engage.'

'No engagement. Understood.' The pilot relayed the new orders to the remaining Hind gunships. 'They're on their way.'

Udlov considered his options. Shooting down an intruder was one thing. Attacking a rescue mission was another.

Had he got to the men first, the Americans' hands would have been tied. They would have had to have been prepared to follow inland, exposing themselves to the SAMs. This was different.

'Do not fire unless attacked.'

'Understood,' the pilot repeated.

While the Apaches and the Hinds stood off against each other in the dark, the Blackhawks landed.

The Marines jumped off and fanned out quickly, forming a protective screen about the RV.

*   *   *

'Captain Adderly?' a Marine lieutenant said to Garner. 'Lieutenant Corinni, sir. We've come to take you home.' Another Marine was with him. 'This is the doc.'

'Very pleased to see you, gentlemen. I'm Garner,' Garner was thankful for the darkness, so they wouldn't see his sorrow. 'Captain Adderly's just here. He's dead.'

The doctor immediately went to Adderly's body to check it.

'I'm sorry, sir,' Corinni said with deep sympathy. 'A fire-fight?'

'No. The SAM got him.'

The six gunships, monstrous dragonflies in the night, hung motionless, their rotors beating an ominous war cry at one another.

'What are they doing?' Udlov asked the pilot.

'Just sitting there,' came the response in his helmet. 'They're out of gun range, so they must have missiles. We are carrying none. They have almost certainly already picked their targets. We'd be out of the sky before we got near. What should we do?'

'Can you get an infrared picture? See if they really are carrying missiles.'

'I can,' It was the co-pilot/gunner who replied.

Seconds later Udlov was viewing the expanded picture of one of the Apaches. It bristled with missiles.

'Well, we know,' Udlov commented drily. 'We do exactly what they're doing. It's a stand-off. As they're carrying missiles, it's obvious they don't want to start a fight any more than we do in this situation. No one wants to escalate. They got there first. We stay here until they leave, just in case.'

Udlov still felt admiration for his opponents in the Eagle. They were an excellent and combative crew. He wouldn't have minded a return match one day.

Whoever they were, they'd managed to evade capture during the day, and were now about to make it back.

From the Americans' point of view, it had been a good haul. Two Su-27Ks down, one damaged; the base compromised, a student pilot dead, and a reputation severely dented.

From my point of view, he thought grimly, it's all downhill if I let Ongg have his way.

But Ongg would not have it his own way. It was time to talk seriously to the lieutenant colonel.

'The Apaches are leaving,' the pilot announced.

'They've picked up their people,' Udlov said. 'Nothing more we can do here. Back to base.'

Dempsey grabbed the phone as soon as it rang.

'We got them!' the Marine colonel's voice said in his ear.

'Good news! Good news!'

'It's not all good, Colonel.'

Dempsey went very still.

Shelley Hoag watched him closely, attempting to gauge the nature of the rest of the news by his reaction. But he was remaining impassive. When he'd finished, he put the phone down so slowly that she feared the worst.

'They've picked them up,' Dempsey told her.

She began to beam; then the beam faltered, then vanished altogether as she saw the pain in his eyes.

'Adderly's dead,' he said bluntly.

He thrust his hands in his pockets and went to stand by a window to look out at the lights of the airfield.

'Garner is totally wrecked by it,' he continued without looking round. 'He did his best to save him, but Adderly had serious internal injuries. They were holed up in a cave that Garner found.

If they hadn't been forced to stay in that damn hole all day, medical attention would have saved Adderly. Goddamit! I didn't want to lose that boy. I didn't want to lose either of them.'

'This is not your fault, sir.'

'It's somebody's. Might as well be me.'

Shelley Hoag did not argue with him, knowing it would be the very worst thing she could do. Like all strong commanders, he outwardly gave the impression he would mercilessly push his men to their limits and beyond. Inside, they always feared losing them. Like those same commanders, he would come to terms with it eventually, and in his own way. But for now, this was his time to give vent to his pain and anger.

'They got *two* Su-27s,' Dempsey went on, sounding as if it was a private conversation with himself. A note of pride had crept in. 'Maybe even a third. And they did the job they were sent out to do. Knew those boys were good. Hell, they got me and Carter in one hop. We lost one hell of a pilot today. We'd better make sure we don't lose one of the best damn wizzos around too. Those boys deserve medals. I'll see that they get them.'

Suddenly, Dempsey whirled and Shelley

Hoag was shocked by the haunted look in his eyes.

'Damn it, Major. We could have saved him! We *should* have!' The haunted eyes remained fastened upon Shelley Hoag. 'I'd like to be alone.'

'Sir,' she said, saluted him, and left the room.

In one of the Blackhawks, Garner sat with his hand on Adderly's body. The Marine doctor had gently tried to move the hand. In the subdued internal lighting the doctor had taken one look at Garner's eyes and had left well alone.

As the Blackhawk, leading the other three helicopters, headed back for the ship, they heard him speaking to the body.

'I'm going to transfer to the front seat,' they heard him say softly. 'I hope I can be as good a pilot as you. And I'll take good care of Arlene, cousin. And young John. I promise.'

He looked up from the body of his friend and kinsman, and saw the others staring at him.

He stared right back until eventually they were forced to look away.

The helicopters skimmed the darkened sea, taking their warriors away from the hostile shore.

OTHER TITLES IN SERIES FROM 22 BOOKS

Available now at newsagents and booksellers
or use the order form provided

continued overleaf . . .

All at £4.99

All 22 Books are available at your bookshop, or can be ordered from:

22 Books
Mail Order Department
Little, Brown and Company
Brettenham House
Lancaster Place
London WC2E 7EN

Alternatively, you may fax your order to the above address. Fax number: 0171 911 8100.

Payments can be made by cheque or postal order, payable to Little, Brown and Company (UK), or by credit card (Visa/Access). Do not send cash or currency. UK, BFPO and Eire customers, please allow 75p per item for postage and packing, to a maximum of £7.50. Overseas customers, please allow £1 per item.

While every effort is made to keep prices low, it is sometimes necessary to increase cover prices at short notice. 22 Books reserves the right to show new retail prices on covers which may differ from those previously advertised in the books or elsewhere.

NAME ....

ADDRESS ....

....

....

☐ I enclose my remittance for £_____
☐ I wish to pay by Access/Visa

Card number
☐☐☐☐ ☐☐☐☐ ☐☐☐☐ ☐☐☐☐

Card expiry date
☐☐ ☐☐

Please allow 28 days for delivery. Please tick box if you do not wish to receive any additional information ☐